OUTLAW BLUES

Paul Williams, "rock critic," was born on January 30, 1966, at the age of seventeen. His birth was self-induced; another part of him had willfully succumbed to the urge to publish and edit, and had started *Crawdaddy!*, "The Magazine of Rock 'n' Roll." He naturally expected the writer side of his personality to aid him in this endeavor by filling the pages of the magazine until other writers could be found. So for the two and one-half years following, my self-expression through writing took the guise of reviews of rock recordings. Fortunately, since no one had fooled around with this particular social function before, I was pretty much able to create my own forms. I want to say that, despite my resentment at being thought of as an expert, I've enjoyed it all. I was born in Boston, Mass., on the 19th of May, 1948, at seven in the evening (Taurus with a Libra moon, Scorpio rising), and I am now living in northern California.

OUTLAW BLUES

A Book of Rock Music

PAUL WILLIAMS

New York
E. P. DUTTON & CO., INC.
1969

Published simultaneously in Canada by
Clarke, Irwin & Company Limited, Toronto and Vancouver.

Library of Congress Catalog Card Number: 69-14857

Second Printing September 1969

This book is for Larry McCombs and Larry Stark

Acknowledgments

My thanks go to the following for permission to use their photographs in this book. All rights are reserved by these photographers:

> Ken Greenberg for photos of Grace Slick, David
> Crosby, Roger McGuinn, and Peter Townshend.
> Elliott Landy for photo of Bob Dylan.
> David Flooke for photo of Bob Weir.
> Elektra Records for photo of The Doors.
> Linda Eastman for photo of Brian Wilson.

Most of the material published in this book was first printed in *Crawdaddy!* Magazine.

I would like to thank David G. Hartwell, who by reading and commenting on the essays as they were written, effectively edited this book.

Contents

Preface   11

1: OUTLAW BLUES   15

2: BLESHING   41

Sunshine Superman
Buffalo Springfield
The Byrds' Greatest Hits and Others

3: TOM PAINE HIMSELF   59

Understanding Dylan
The Period of Silence
God Bless America

4: WHAT WENT ON   81

5: THE NIGHT ON FIRE   93

Rock Is Rock: A Discussion of a Doors Song
Rothchild Speaks

6: BRIAN   117

A Celebration of *Wild Honey*
The Tragedy of *Smile*

7: HOW ROCK COMMUNICATES   171

Discography   189
Bibliography   190
Recommended Reading   190
Rock for Beginners   190
Background   191
7

Illustrations

Grace Slick of Jefferson Airplane   14

David Crosby of The Byrds   40

Roger McGuinn of The Byrds   40

Bob Dylan   58

Bob Weir of The Grateful Dead   80

The Doors   92

Brian Wilson   116

Peter Townshend of The Who   170

9

Preface

This book is not what you think it is; and maybe if I say it right out like that you'll believe me. Most people see rock as a phenomenon; by that logic I should write a report, an explanation or exposition of this phenomenon. A nice book telling you what rock is and what it does and how. But rock to me is not a phenomenon at all—if it is, that fact is not significant—rather I see rock as a means of expression, an opportunity for beauty, an art. So what I have written is expression, not explanation; an attempt to convey what I feel from the music, an exploration of what rock does to me. Reading the book will not "explain" the music to you; but it might bring you closer to the music, and closer to me. And perhaps the experience of reading it will better enable you to "explain" rock to yourself.

". . . And everybody here listen to my song tonight; gonna save the whole world" (Mick Jagger).

OUTLAW BLUES

Grace Slick of Jefferson Airplane.
Photo by Ken Greenberg.

1: OUTLAW BLUES

December 1967

"I wish I was on some Australian mountain range. . . ."

People who work in mass media are supposed to be half manipulator and half prophet; and all around the mulberry bush now producers, performers, and persons who just like to rap are wondering about the Future of Rock (and roll). They talk about stuff like the following:

During 1967 rock music, thanks to Beatles Doors Airplane etc., greatly expanded its audience to the point where maybe two-thirds of the people buying any records at all were buying rock albums. Meanwhile, also thanks to Beatles Doors Airplane etc., the number of creative musicians and groups within the field grew even faster. Situation: during the summer of 1967, by some awesome coincidence, the size and interests of the buying audience coincided nicely with the quantity and quality of rock albums newly available to them, and hence the considerable success of people like Jimi Hendrix, Country Joe & the Fish, the Doors, the Mothers, Moby Grape, and so on. Lots of creative people making it pretty big with creative stuff, and this in turn led to unrestrained enthusiasm on the part of large record companies, who've been spending unbelievable amounts to make sure that any group that sounds talented to them will in the future record on their label. In the same manner, successful groups have pushed and shoved their way into the studios, sparing no expense, taking as much time and using as many tools as might seem necessary to really Do What They Want To Do. Because it looks like the enthusiasm of the audience for good stuff will make it all worthwhile.

15

But already in December 1967 the difficulties are becoming apparent. For one thing, there are quite a number of good groups making records, and they all expect a slice of the pie. Can the same audience that—phenomenally—put the Beatles, the Doors, the Stones, and Jefferson Airplane in the top five on the lp charts at the same time, can they purchase enough records now to put Donovan, Love, Country Joe, Judy Collins, the Rolling Stones, the Beatles, the Beach Boys, Van Dyke Parks, the Hollies, Paul Butterfield, Jefferson Airplane, the Incredible String Band, and Buffalo Springfield in the top five at the same time? All of the above have released new albums in the last month, as I write this, and the Who, the Kinks, Moby Grape, the Byrds, Jimi Hendrix, Randy Newman, the Grateful Dead, the Mothers, and the Velvet Underground have stuff scheduled for the immediate future. Elbow room! cried Dan'l Boone. Every one of these groups expects to be able to spend $50,000 or more recording an album, and if this much good stuff is going to be released every two months, who's going to pay for it?

The immediate answer is clear: expand the audience. But since we've already moved in on most of the existent music audience, this means a very heavy undertaking: we have to increase the number of people who are actually listening to and buying any music at all. We have to not only show why rock music is good music, but why Music Itself Is Good For You and so on and on. And maybe even the quantity of really good stuff being released nowadays will help us do it.

But there's one word back there you might have overlooked. *Coincidence*. What if it suddenly turns out that what Country Joe & the Fish (or even the Beatles) feel like doing with all that expensive recording-time freedom is not the same thing as what our dear expanding audience wants to listen to? What if good creative art is not always appreciated by huge numbers of people the instant it's available?

That's What People Are Talking About, folks. And it's all fairly relevant to the albums at hand. The Beach Boys, a group that class prejudice prevents many of us from appreciating, released in the summer of 1966 an album called *Pet Sounds,* to me one of the very finest rock albums of all time. It was not exactly Far*Out, but it was kinda subtle compared to the previous Beach Boys stuff; and partly for that reason, and mostly because of timing, *Pet Sounds* was the first Beach Boys album in several years *not* to be a million-seller. The timing factor was one not unfamiliar to us in 1967—the big hit on the album, "Sloop John B," made it in December 1965, but because of the amount of studio time required to do the album right, *Pet Sounds* wasn't released till June and lost its impact as a result. And the mere fact that the record was really beautiful wasn't enough to salvage the situation. Fans don't always care about that.

But the fans *loved* the group's previous album, *Beach Boys Party,* a million-seller which most of us heavy rock listeners looked down upon as a sloppy, drunken recording of moldy oldies from 1961. Not even good (we thought then) in the context of the Beach Boys, let alone as a Rock Album. Yet the record sold terrifically, despite its dollar-extra price (a gala gatefold presentation) and the fact that there was another Beach Boys album, released just before it, competing for the fans' attention.

So maybe Beach Boys fans are stupid, and we can dismiss the whole thing. But maybe that's a pretty snotty attitude to take; maybe something is happening here that we just ought to know about. *Beach Boys Party* is an excellent album containing excellent music *that is easy to relate to*! And that's why the fans dug it, dug it more than that other excellent lp *Pet Sounds,* and that's the real reason people buy records—not because they're dupes, but because they like music, and the better it is the more they like it as long as they are still able to relate to what's good about it.

Not that I want to say that if lots of people like something, it's good. We all know what Humpty Dumpty said, and since I'm the one who's stuck with whatever definition of the word

I care to accept, I'll feel more comfortable believing it's "good" if I feel it is rather than it's "good" if it wins the popularity polls. But we are talking about the relationship between what a performer feels like doing and what a large audience—large enough to pay for that performer's studio time—feels like listening to. So the extent to which large bunches of people are able to relate to things is pretty important.

I said the *Beach Boys Party* album is excellent, and I was talking about my own subjective response, of course. Yet that's an educated response—i.e., in 1965 I didn't like the record, I really put it down, and now after two more years of listening to rock intensively I feel that the album is a very good one. My opinion now is probably more valid than my opinion then—not because of any directionality of time but because I'm writing for an audience of people most of whom have also listened to a great deal of rock in the last two years. They can relate to my present point of view, at least in terms of common experience.

Let's drop this for a moment. Do you like the new Stones album? I hope you do. I went through a period of about a week (after loving it initially) where I was really unsure if I liked it or not. I liked many parts of it, but I wasn't quite comfortable with the whole thing. I stuck with it, of course—there hasn't been a Rolling Stones album yet I've disliked, after giving it a little time to sink in—and pretty soon I lost my uneasiness, so that now I am quite convinced it's a great record, and I'm at a loss to explain my moments of doubt. Sometimes you have to listen to a record for a while before you can accept it on its own ground. And the *quantity* of good stuff coming out this month might have made me doubt my good judgment. Anyway, happy ending.

The Stones always come through. I didn't like *Flowers* at first, and now I realize how incredibly difficult it was to design an album so unpresuming that it could be released in June 1967 and not be compared to *Sergeant Pepper*. After the initial shock of seeing two songs on *Flowers* that were on the previous album, and realizing that the rest of the record was a chaotic assortment of rejects from *Buttons, Aftermath,* and *The Rolling Stones Sing Motown,* I now listen to the record with great pleasure, I feel that "Ride On Baby" is surely one of the great rock songs and that the Stones, faced with the problem (among others) of releasing some great 1966 songs in 1967, met the situation head-on with a thoroughly successful anachronistic album. And the fans didn't care (another million-seller). Only the critics were ruffled.

The Stones always come through. It's not a coincidence. I remember in 1965 I just assumed that you couldn't judge a song the first few times you heard it. "Satisfaction" felt great the first time through, but I couldn't *hear* anything at all. Piece by piece the structure of the song, as I listened again and again, came clear to me from all that confusion. "Get Off of My Cloud" sounded like pure noise the first ten times through on a transistor radio. The form of a song is something you see all at once. When it comes to you, you suddenly find a picture of the entire song in your head, and at any given point you're aware of the context, the whole thing. Until you get that picture, you just follow a line through the song—you hear something, you hear something else, finally the song is over. The more you listen, the more you begin to sense a shape replacing that line, until eventually the song is familiar to you and you're not lost any more ("gestalt perception"—you can perceive a thing as part of a group, you can perceive a group as a collection of things).

And it's not a coincidence. Because the one thing the Stones are absolute masters of—and it certainly shows on the new album—is structure. If you take the Rolling Stones and maroon them in the swirling vacuum of space, stranded with nothing but ether, that imponderable stuff of the universe, to play with, they'll take that ether and mold it into a space ship and come chasing back after you, and they're the only rock group that can do that.

Again and again, not just on this album but throughout

their procession of not-quite-a-dozen albums, the Rolling Stones incorporate chaos by creating entirely new structures out of it, and never are they incoherent. If you listen to a Stones song long enough you'll *always* see the picture, always perceive the whole and feel relaxed at the naturalness of it all . . . no matter how much of a struggle it was for you to break through to that naturalness.

And the Stones love to fool around. They sound sloppy—they don't want you to feel comfortable till you get there. They give the impression of incoherence so that their uptight listeners will buzz off and not bother them, and so the people who care will not relax on the surface but will continue to penetrate the song until they've really got to it. "Open our minds let the pictures come. . . ."

This applies not only to songs, but to albums. *Their Satanic Majesties Request* sounds like a wild assortment of stuff the first time you hear it, and ends up being a monolith. Having a brand new Rolling Stones album in your hands is like being a virgin, on the brink. The first rush is ecstatic. And when you finally get *there*, you marvel at the Stones, you can't believe they've really done it again, you're overcome with the sense of wonder. Sure feels good.

And feeling good, let's wallow around in the album awhile, since that's what's fun in a review. Take a song and notice some things about it, petty pleasantries, universal truths, anything to give us that nice feeling that we're all listening to the same songs and hearing something like the same sort of thing.

"Sing This All Together" is a nice idea. I don't want to get too involved in comparing it with the idea of *Sergeant Pepper*, because I really don't think they have much in common—on the surface they do (in fact, both concepts hark back to the end of *Between the Buttons*), but it's immediately apparent that the Lonely Hearts Club Band is a structural convenience, a cute outer shell, whereas "Sing This All Together" is a musical and emotional concept in which every track on the album is deeply involved. *Sergeant Pepper* isn't a very significant musical influence on *Satanic Majesties*—it's an experiential influence. That is, the Beatles took the Stones on a *Sergeant Pepper* trip, and the Stones returned and created this album. The audience, too, obviously listens to *Satanic Majesties* in the context of just having lived with *Sergeant Pepper* for lo, these several months, and thus the experience of the Beatles album is a strong influence on both the people who recorded the Stones lp, and the people who are listening to it. *Satanic Majesties* is influenced by but does not resemble *Sergeant Pepper*.

On page two of any British passport is a sentence which starts, "Her Britannic Majesty . . . requests and requires," etc.

And "Citadel" is about New York City. I read that in the *New Musical Express*. But it's really about Fritz Lang's *Metropolis*, a 1926 science-fiction flick envisioning City of the Future, with huge evil buildings run by steam, nightmare machines, and tiny people running every which way. The broken reentry in the middle of the song is kind of like the entire musical history of the Who in one half of a note; and maybe Candy and Taffy know that it can be pretty nice to live in a citadel. But if you've seen Mick stand there on stage after the girls have broken through the cop line, you know he doesn't want to be protected.

Oh, well, as Mick says toward the end of "Citadel." Bill Wyman is probably the only Stone who could have written a Gilbert (tarantara!) & Sullivan rock song. But the best thing about "In Another Land" is the tremendous sense of relief each time the sleeper wakes and finds himself surrounded by the Rolling Stones, drums, chorus, and all. In fact, no matter how far into the dim recesses of outer space this album may take you, you always get the comforting feeling that the Stones are right there beside you, and the situation's completely under control. Things may seem to be getting out of hand—look at all that stuff on the front cover of the jacket—but the bored faces of the Stones remind you once again that it's all right.

And this certainly is a science-fiction album. While Bill Wyman, Jimi Hendrix, and Grace Slick were home reading each other's comic books, Mick and Keith must have been down at the movies, digging Robbie the Robot in *Forbidden Planet*. *Their Satanic Majesties Request* is full of ancient empires based on decimal computers, and monsters from behind the Id. Sandy Pearlman may think the Byrds sing about the way the earth turns, Bill Wyman in Wonderland accidentally wonders "Is this some kind of (cosmic) joke?" but Mick and Keith *know* that Old Sol (our mr. sun) is the best we can do for a local center of activity, and they never wonder where the yellow went. "Sun turning round with graceful motion." Solipsism is for the byrds. "Pictures of us spin the circling sun." Bill Wyman's probably afraid to close all his eyes together, by this time.

"2000 Man" is like the Incredible String Band's "Back in the 1960's." The structure of the song is breathtaking, a further step along the trail blazed by the Association with "Windy." And the phrase "don't you know I'm a 2000 man?" reflects an absolute mastery of rock lyrics.

A good thing, too, for the next track is an instrumental, sort of a "Now I've Got a Witness" (Stones album one, if your memory is failing) for "Sing This All Together"—a true Nanker Phelge creation. "Sing This All Together (See What Happens)" is my favorite track on an album that doesn't really have favorite tracks. Some people think it's silly, but they're wrong. It's even possible that "See What Happens" is influenced by "Goin' Home" via Love's "Revelation," which would be magnificent, but that's not important. What is important is that there's always something going on in this mosaic, and it's always not-quite-familiar and always worthwhile. See, the nice thing is not that they're doing "this kind of stuff"—any old Pink Floyd or John Fahey can do this kind of stuff, but in the case of the Stones the stuff itself is incredible. Brilliant raw music, the same stuff as very early rock and roll but without the words or much of the instrumentation. The same Music, though, don't you see? The Rolling Stones' instincts are absolutely musical, and that's one of the reasons they can't do anything wrong.

D. G. Hartwell points out that the reprise at the end of "See What Happens" is an electronic "We Wish You a Merry Christmas." And it's worth noting that in terms of timing and impact, this is the first Christmas album since *Rubber Soul*.

"She's a Rainbow" is a popular crowd-pleaser; and it's kind of relevant to our whole theme here to discuss how the Stones manage to keep turning out hit singles. Pretty melodies—this one reminds me of "Never on Sunday"—help, of course, but mostly I think they make it because they know how to knock people out and make them feel comfortable at the same time. "She's a Rainbow" *is* easy to relate to. It sounds like a song the very first time you hear it, and anyone can tell it's about how nice this girl is. So there aren't any obstacles to the casual listener's enjoyment of the song . . . but that doesn't mean it's superficial. Like "Paint It Black"- or "Ruby Tuesday," "Rainbow" gets you deeper involved each time you hear it. And beneath that secure, surface feeling of order and accessibility, there's a lot of stuff happening here—much too much to immediately resolve and store away in some part of your mind, more than enough to make the song continually fresh and worthwhile. I don't want to pretend I've solved the mystery of what makes a hit record, but I think we can agree that "Rainbow" is the prettiest, and the most accessible, song on the album. That's interesting data.

"The Lantern" is another structural masterpiece, with those incredible sweeping transitions, perfectly placed feedback, echoes, guitar whispers and screams that never intrude, until you suddenly feel part of some exceedingly formal cosmic hopscotch game that has gone on for millennia. The song sounds absolutely right, without sounding like anything that ever was before. It's a Diogenes trip (and Bob Dylan said, "Don't ask me nothin' about nothin'; I just might tell you the truth." But the Stones aren't even afraid of being really serious).

"Gomper" (I'm reading the *New Musical Express* again) is supposed to be "the Tibetan term for the incredible journey some Tibetan monks make while under hypnosis." It sounds like a great outdoors trip to me—some kind of sexual encounter at the beginning, then lots of open meadows, afternoon sunshine, running and smiling, growing things and wildlife and a real sense of wonder. The music, which is just too good to describe, carries you further and further away, till all of a sudden you can't see the place you started from, and the music starts doing little fear things as the pleasure fades, and you're 2000 light-years from home. Which may sound contrived, but it works, over and over again. So the Stones can even create something completely open-ended, and give it that firm feeling of structure.

As for "2000 Light Years," it's really Twilight Zone stuff. Like Manzarek in "The End," the organist creates the whole song in the context of one note (another D. G. Hartwell revelation) while the bass and guitar go through some obscure variations on "Gloria." What you get is this sinuous, ethereal song that really feels like it could absorb dozens of adjectives like that with no trouble at all. And you learn all about the acceptance of alien surroundings. "Gomper"/"2000 Light Years" is really just a very subtle reworking of the theme of "Waterloo Sunset."

Each song on this album is different, but not really separate, from the others; the works are interconnected on almost every level. So you can apply your gestalt perception to the whole album, and this makes "On with the Show" a special pleasure simply because it's the final song. Everything is resolved, and you really feel good about it, like maybe you really did see, for a moment, where we all come from. And the other side of the coin is that "On with the Show" tells you you don't have to take it all too seriously ("Sergeant Pepper Reprise" told you you didn't have to take it all seriously *except* "A Day in the Life"). The way it works in the context of the Stones album is you can get as involved as you like while you're there, while you're listening to it, and you don't have to think about it at all once it's over. It's an experience we all have together, the Stones and us, and it's not meant to have any further significance. The Beatles say they'd "love to take you home with us"; the Stones aren't polite, but they'll "get you safely to your door." What more could you ask?

And the best thing about the cover is that they didn't spoil it by making it *too* good.

Two words are really significant to Jefferson Airplane's sound and appeal: complexity and kinetics. Familiar words, and fairly simple ones. Complexity: there's a lot going on, all the time. Kinetics: the listener is caught up in the motion of the songs. *After Bathing at Baxter's* is the best Jefferson Airplane album, in terms of both overall quality and the extent to which it captures the life style of the group. Had it been released in January 1967, I think it would have been generally recognized as the crowning achievement of the dawn of American rock, 1965–1966, just as *The Rolling Stones Now!* is the summation and peak of the young rock scene in Britain, 1963–1964. The mere fact that *Baxter's* arrived inappropriately in December 1967 does not take away its real importance. This is the album that all us young Byrds, Paul Butterfield, Lovin' Spoonful fans were waiting for.

Waves of "Pooneil," washing over the listener, carrying him back. It's always a nice transition into "Pooneil," from whatever album you were listening to, the cleansing feedback which is almost thematic in *Baxter's* and then that "Memphis" bass & drums opening which will outlive Chuck Berry and all the rest of us. The Stones album is nice to make noises to, blare at the brass parts and just be friendly with, but the Airplane lp is from the good ol' days when you'd move your whole body, or pretend you were playing along with the lead guitar. You can almost see Grace and Marty asking the audience to dance.

The complexity is apparent immediately. The Airplane don't have the inherent sense of structure that has blessed the Rolling Stones, but they know the rules, know them well enough to break them masterfully. "Watch Her Ride" and "Won't You Try/Saturday Afternoon" both take off from basic Byrds/Stones/Beatles concepts and then employ such daring and casually self-confident variations (watch what happens to the "watch you ride" phrase, for example) that it takes a while to realize what they're getting away with. Paul Kantner is on the verge of becoming a major rock architect. "Pooneil" is a stunning achievement, a five-minute song that flows as one line (with a loop) from beginning to end, never stopping long enough to let the listener see it as a static shape.

Complexity. In "Pooneil" Paul and Marty trade off lead vocals, sometimes sing together and sometimes sing together with Grace. Grace also has one brief solo moment, and may even act as a second voice to Paul or Marty. So you have vocals by A, B, A&B, A&B&C, C, A&C, and B&C. In addition to which Grace acts as a sort of shadow throughout the song, repeating what the lead voice sings in her own very special I-am-a-background-instrument style. Since the last album Grace has really gotten into the art of group vocals, and—like everyone else in the group she can't do the simplest thing without being clever and individualistic and creative about it—this really adds to the richness of the Airplane sound.

Complexity. So many personalities, and each completely independent of the others; each man integrating his music into the whole thing, but also using his instrument as a means to impose his personal style on whatever's going down.

When the Stones do a song, there's some general feeling of "this is how it's gonna be," and while each musician's style is apparent and important, it's pretty well understood that the song should express whatever the songwriters had in mind. With the Airplane, the songwriter is considered just one of six group members, and so a song like "Wild Tyme" is created by a sort of committee consisting of one songwriter, three vocalists, a bass player, a drummer, a solo guitarist, a rhythm guitarist, and a guy with a tambourine. It sometimes takes a while to get all these heads together (seven months, in the case of this album), but in the end there is a real musical confluence, a feeling on the part of every group member that everything's in place.

But it wouldn't be very important *how* the music was created, were it not for the fact that you can hear the difference with your very own ears. A Stones song is listened to as a song, and you pretty much feel you hear the whole thing every time. Sometimes it doesn't hit you as hard as other times, but it's all there. With an Airplane song, it's very easy to hear different stuff each time you listen. Try it. Listen to "Wild Tyme," and then listen to it again concentrating just on what the lead guitar is doing. Then dig the rhythm guitar, the interaction between Paul on rhythm and Jorma on lead and the huge differences between the two guitarists even when they're playing essentially the same part. The personalities of these musicians come through very clear in their playing—they aren't self-conscious, nothing is held back, it's all there for the listener to groove on. Pay attention to what the drums are doing. Try to feel the movement of the bass guitar, which is really buried on this track. Listen to the vocal very carefully, trying to pick out the quieter things that are happening. Listen for the separate personalities of the vocalists in the harmony parts. Pick up on the *way* each word is mouthed. There's a lot going on.

And you don't have to put in a lot of conscious effort to enjoy all this. One of the reasons the Airplane album is so fresh, so endlessly attractive, is that you do hear new stuff each time you listen. You can't help it—there are an awful lot of specifics on this album, crying out to be heard and appreciated, and they'll jump out at you no matter how you ignore them. Despite "Two Heads" being mostly Grace's song, with a heavy emphasis on her friend the percussionist, sooner or later you're sure to discover the sweetness of the bass part, the brilliance of what Jack is doing in there. The joy of complexity, when the music is good, is that every pleasure is pushed further by the constant discovery of yet *another* great thing going on, and there's just too much music, appreciable on too many levels, for it ever to grow tiresome. The sheer fun of the music is increased sixfold by the extent to which everyone's into it.

"Pooneil" is the masterpiece, every moment orchestrated, every musician loving it. And with all that activity, it's still just a Pooh trip: there wasn't That Much to learn out today, but it sure does feel better knowing it. Just another day, and who but the Airplane could get so much out of it? Who but JA would say "armadillo"?

"A Small Package of Value Will Come to You, Shortly" is great ad lib theatre, stretched and structured by the cleverness of the concertmaster and his tape recorder and his percussion collection. Spencer reaches out, grabs "Pooneil" with one hand, "Young Girl Sunday Blues" with the other, and ties them together with a wonderful word bath in concentric and overlapping circles, "Joy to the World" in the center for punctuation. The closer you listen to this, the more you like it; what makes the Airplane or the Stones more important than so many other clever people is that their cleverness holds up under inspection, in fact turns out to be real valid groovy music. And it's nice to be so careful without ever being too cautious.

"Young Girl Sunday Blues" is a pleasure: real Marty Balin lyrics, such as you don't hardly find anymore. Mick's great "Don't you know I'm a 2000 man?" is equaled and surpassed by Marty's "Don't you know [careful emphasis on each of the three words] what I have found—maybe you've found it too?" Not that either of these guys really wants to get into the social psychology of knowledge, or whatever; it's just that so much in rock depends on the singer's attitude toward the listener. Mick assumes absolutely nothing, so he can cheerfully pretend his audience knows everything, even things they might not know *how* to know. But Marty takes his listeners very seriously, and don't think "young and new" girls don't appreciate that. And what has Marty found? "Today is made up of yesterday and tomorrow—young girl Sunday blues and all her sorrow." Can you honestly say you didn't know *that*?

But I'm not kidding when I say I think Marty is the best lyricist in Airplane. Paul has a really nice feeling for words that don't mean very much, but Marty is just rational enough and just irrational enough to really set you free. "So much can be heard," he sings, and Jorma just goes right on playing "Get Out of My Life Woman" on his guitar.

Paul Kantner has David Crosby's rhythm and Gene Clark's mind. But none of these three guys is a member of the Byrds. "Martha she keeps her heart in a broken clock" ("she'll always be there, my love don't care about time"). "I didn't know you were the one for me, I couldn't see, but you were waiting" ("I have never been so far out in front that I could ask for what I want and have it any time"). John Kelehor told me about Crosby's incredible rhythm, and he should know (Byrd-for-a-day). But John also sat in for John Densmore in Portland recently; and Paul Rothchild and I both agree that Paul Kantner is one of the few people in the world who could be a Door. I only bring this up because Paul K. thinks *Crawdaddy!* is too serious a magazine sometimes, and I wanted to show that we are.

And "Martha" is a pretty song. Unlike the Stones, the Airplane finds nothing mysterious in the great outdoors. Instead, they're comfortable enough to do verbal acrobatics ("she weeds a part through a token lock," very nice) and pull off a Lear Jet eggshell landing near the end. Everybody slows down, and Jorma is very careful; Paul recites, and the opening of "Wild Tyme" at that moment is about as perfect as anything on the album, or anywhere else.

"Wild Tyme" mostly borrows words from other songs on *Baxter's,* but that's okay for a genuine rave-up in the Yardbirds' "Strolling On" *Blow-Up* tradition. "I'm here for you any old time," and that's the Airplane—accessible.

Jorma's song is an assault, but it comes after so much other stuff that the listener is practically numb. I like the auto accident in the middle.

And there's more to the Airplane than accessibility. But their only air of mystery comes from their being so obvious on the surface (the words of the songs) and yet always so perceptibly better-than-obvious. It's always been a source of confusion to me that I get so much pleasure from the over-familiar lyrics of "Today" or "Blues from an Airplane"— there must be more going on than the obvious, stereotyped stuff, or why do I like it so much? And Sandy's article on Jefferson Airplane's use of the cliché (*Crawdaddy!* 9) by no means answers all my questions. Because Sandy doesn't really like Marty's lyrics; he only appreciates them.

Grace, in fact, sometimes suffers by seeming less obvious than the rest of the group. "White Rabbit" came on with an air of mystery, but was so utterly decipherable that, for me, it rapidly lost its impact. "Pooneil" pretends to no mystery at all, but the more you listen to it the more subtle it seems. Something's happening here. Grace's songs on this new album are both very good, easy to respect, but hard to really get into. There's no place to hide. When you wonder if "Two Heads" is about hypocrisy, the double standard, you do that on a very intellectual level. As you listen more, you don't get involved in the song; instead you get hung up in the very interesting, very exciting things that she does with her voice. Maybe you groove on the instrumentation. But you groove on its quality more than on any particular emotion it might inspire. Grace makes everyone, especially herself, a studio musician.

That isn't a put-down. But I think we're all aware of the good qualities of stuff like "rejoyce" and "Two Heads," and it's strange that the area in which Grace falls down is exactly that thing that the Airplane as a whole does best, the conjuring of emotions out of motion and involvement. Grace's stuff is not exactly static, but fluid—her singing has no real motion, since motion really cannot be divorced from the idea of movement in a direction, but rather flows from place to place without covering any ground to speak of. This is confusing. You can hear what I mean by listening to "rejoyce." ". . . I got his arm . . . I got his arm . . . I've had it for weeks . . . I got his arm Stephen won't give his arm to no gold-star mother's farm war's good business so give your son and I'd rather have my country die for me!" Even from the words you can see that she shifts from phrase to phrase without any apparent sense of overall direction. When you listen, you'll see that she also does it with absolutely no hesitation, shifting emotions timelessly from pleasure and possessiveness to pride, a sort of stark innocence, warm female sensitivity, righteousness and derision and finally anger building to fury. If you tried to clock her speed in moving from one emotion to the next, you'd feel pretty silly, for she doesn't move in time in the sense that "Pooneil" or "Young Girl Sunday" moves. She merely shifts, now I'm here, now over here, now somewhere else, like that. In "Two Heads," toward the end, she flows like liquid on some nonabsorbent surface, splattering by sheer will power. This is the sort of thing we mortals can only sit back and watch, and maybe that's just as well. "Rejoyce," which used to be and should have been called "Ulysses," is a detached "work of art," not flawless but certainly impressive, and that's Grace doing all that fine piano and recorder stuff. The last line is regrettably unintelligible; reliable sources inform me she's saying "but somehow it all falls apart." She sure is cynical.

In opposition to this, we have Jefferson Airplane, including Grace as a harmony voice, with their incredible Airplane kineticism. Kineticism all started in rock 'n' roll with the basic desire to get the audience off their feet and dancing. So you employ every trick you know to make your listeners not just feel each beat, but feel the succession of beats, feel them more and more until they anticipate each beat and throw their bodies into it. And then you discover some simple devices that accent each movement even more than the audience expects, so that no matter how much they're moving, the song says, "Faster! Harder!" and pretty soon the people have forgotten all about the individual notes or beats and they're just moving with you, entirely caught up in the music.

There's a lot of technique that goes into kineticism, and none of the people who are best at it—the Who ("Anyway, Anyhow, Anywhere"), the Kinks ("Milk Cow Blues"), Them ("Mystic Eyes"), the Four Tops ("Reach Out, I'll Be There")—need to think about it very much. They strain to make the music move, and it moves. It moves because the singer holds back a little on the vocal while the music tries to plunge ahead, which is something like sitting on a ticking bomb. It moves because the bass and drums set up a powerful rhythmic constancy and then the rhythm guitar starts coming in on the beat, but just a tiny fraction late, pulling the listener ahead of the music. Tension is established. And once you've got a little tension, then you just make things a little louder and a little faster, harder, louder, faster, harder, faster, harder, louder, faster, faster, boom! More than one listener has had his head blown off by kinetic resolution.

Airplane kineticism won't blow your head off, but it should get you excited—it's high quality roller-coaster stuff. "Watch Her Ride" is high kinetics—the first two verses run along with Paul, Jack, and Spencer building it up nicely, Jorma hinting at better things to come with his truncated solo runs off to one side. Things break loose after "for me" in the second verse. Single guitar notes, punctuated by bass runs, are used as waves of sound, each wave rising from the crest of the one previous.

Vocals break in on the fourth wave and sustain both the wave motion and the feeling of building intensity, while Jorma allows himself the luxury of three or even four notes to drive the vocals harder. The word phrases themselves are kinetic— "times don't change" moves into "times don't ever change"; "the only thing in my world, the only thing that my mind could find for love for love and peace of mind for me . . . for me." Grace's gliding solo on "for me" carries the force of this section nicely into the third verse of the song.

Kineticism is very much a group thing—if everyone in the band doesn't cooperate and work toward the same end, nothing will happen. But the single most important contributor to the kineticism of the Airplane is the interaction between lead guitar and bass. Jack and Jorma have been playing together since long before the formation of the Airplane; they understand each other's music and work together with a closeness that is unusual to rock. They tie the group together, because the musical ground between bass and lead guitar is such that drums, rhythm guitar, and vocals can fit right into whatever motion is going on between them. The complexity of the group is likewise based on this bond; in the end, it is only the alliance between Jack and Jorma that allows one unified piece of music to emerge as the product of six highly individual minds.

The Casady-Kaukonen relationship is explored in depth on *Baxter's* in a jam guitar/bass/drums jam entitled "Spare Chaynge." Jefferson Airplane is fearless in a pleasantly insignificant way: they're not afraid of stuffing an album with good unaesthetic doodling (on the inside sleeve), photos that don't look like them (the centerfold), bad puns ("Spare Chaynge," "rejoyce," "How Suite It Is"), structureless nine-minute jam sessions, etc. Sometimes they really are ballsy in their pointless fearlessness. By making the "suites"—two or three songs segued together—look like single tracks, they make it extremely difficult for any dj to play individual songs off the album. This in spite of the fact that it is easy—the

Rolling Stones did it—to link the songs with spiral grooves that will both make the music continuous and make the individual songs identifiable to anyone looking at the disk. In other words, the Airplane has the balls to stand up to dj's even for no reason at all.

The way to listen to the jam is position yourself before the speakers so that Jack is on one side, Jorma is on the other, and Spencer is somewhere in the middle. By consciously listening to what each guy is doing in relation to the others, you can really get at the heart of this track—it's a dance, a ballet interaction between three persons. And interpretation is entirely up to the listener. The piece starts—for me—with hesitation, not much music, kind of an uptight scene that has to be loosened for anything to happen. Jack assumes the burden of getting things going—he works at getting Jorma involved in the music, he hesitates, tries one tack, then another, never pushes too hard, plays very gently as he starts to get Jorma's interest, kindling the spark . . . Jorma loosens up under this foreplay, tries a run or two, still isn't quite comfortable—but he's coming alive. Spencer withdraws when he sees the tension of the situation, and the importance of leaving the two of them alone until Jack gets Jorma going. Jorma really starts to unwind, plays something nice, Jack coaxes him along, Jorma stops, comes back with a really satisfying thing, gets completely involved in his playing, almost immediately Jack lets loose for the first time, Spencer comes back in with dignity once the ice has been broken, and now, four minutes into the track, real music is happening. Music as an interaction, a conversation analogous to an intellectual or sexual meeting of minds, but separate from them, something that only musicians can experience. "Spare Chaynge" is, for me, a vicarious thrill, an exciting presentation of not music as external art, intended to reach some sort of audience, but music as personal, internal communication and understanding between three people. A jam like all others—but so clear, so easy-to-relate-to that it becomes one of the most important pieces of music in a long while.

Which leaves us with "Won't You Try," only one of the most optimistic performances in the history of rock and roll. The Airplane, despite everything, have absolute confidence in their audience. It's kind of like the early American preacher, in front of his congregation, looking out at the faces of every worst kind of sinner, and knowing that every last mother's son of them is going to be saved. It makes no difference at all that Paul Kantner said, in "Watch Her Ride," "Times don't ever change for me." Now the only truth—and it's noble, glorious, exultant—is this: "Times can change. It's what I say is true. All is real, and I'll come through for you." It doesn't even make much sense, but you know he means every word of it. They all do. You don't have to listen to the words—this song is the peak of the Airplane in terms of expressing pure emotion through complexity, loudness, movement. Every conceivable thing is going on, and it comes through as straightforward and plain as could be. If you're in any kind of good spirits, this song·will raise them through the roof. And isn't that what we really want from rock music?

That's what we get from the Beach Boys. *Beach Boys Party* is a friendly, pleasant record, recorded by people who really understand the common ground between "Papa-Ooom-Mow-Mow," "Mountain of Love," and "The Times They Are A-Changin'." "It's *all* rock," as R. Meltzer or anybody would say, and the Beach Boys really know what that means. It means this is music that's "here for you any old time," and that means you if you're a performer pleasantly fooling around at a party, or you if you're a kid camping out at Big Sur with a baby phonograph and a copy of "Light My Fire."

And you've got to give the Beach Boys credit (especially if you don't want to). Because this album was recorded two and a half years ago, and it's full of the sort of understanding that most rock performers are just beginning to get into.

Street noises were nice before John Cage put his signature on them; and what's the difference if the Beach Boys really *had* a party, and the Stones just pretended to have one?

I mean, I'm talking about the perception of things. It's all in how you see it. In *Crawdaddy!* 11 we ran a centerfold of Jim Morrison, "Cancel My Subscription to the Resurrection." It was sort of designed as a poster, but we didn't indicate that in the magazine, because we thought it might sound silly. So a lot of people thought it was a paid ad. Then Jefferson Airplane sent us a thousand dollars, and a two-page ad of group doodling related to their new album. We ran it as a centerfold in number twelve, and naturally it looked like copy; it didn't look like an ad at all. But so what? Both spreads were quite attractive, and does it really matter *which one* brought in some cash to help put out the following issue?

What's important is that our readers enjoyed this stuff. Maybe even got something out of it, on a personal level. And what matters in music is what's there, what's audible and recognizable and "meaningful" in any way whatsoever to the person listening (and to the people playing). Intentions, motivations, circumstances . . . those are for historians. They're interesting, nice to know about, useful and even important, but they don't have to do with the music and the immediacy of listening to it.

And context notwithstanding, the thing that makes *Beach Boys Party* a good album (to me) is the fact that it's nice to listen to. But what makes it an excellent album is that while I'm listening to this record-that-is-nice-to-listen-to, I get a lot of extra stuff: I get moved on an emotional level, I get insight into the nature of rock music and the creative impulse itself, I get impressions of the world and the way people feel about it, I get a lot of just plain good reactions. Stuff that stays with me. And at no added cost, which kind of makes this record better than just any nice-to-listen-to album.

And the same is true of the Stones and Airplane albums, and lots of other stuff. The Beach Boys deserve historical credit for understanding and expressing something (a certain attitude toward music) first, but the value of the record *now* has nothing to do with when it came out. And it's obviously not necessary to read this review in order to appreciate any of these records. It might be nice to listen to some stuff after getting a really detailed look through another person's eyes (ears), but that's a different pleasure. I wrote a whole article in *Crawdaddy!* 11 about the aspects of listening to rock in a particular environment, the extent to which the context can be part of the musical experience. Groovy. Now I want to make it clear as can be that the *creation* of the music is noncontextual, that we've gone beyond the days when rock was specifically designed for everybody's car radio. The musician, the performer, can*not* create music for people in other recording studios, who also have Altex 605 speakers, or whatever, to listen through. He can't become involved only in what his own ears perceive, at the moment of creation and the playback five minutes later.

Or rather, he certainly can. I correct myself. I'd be the last person to urge restrictions on anyone's freedom, and I sincerely believe that creating for an audience of ten, or one, or zero, is just as valid as anything else. Certainly the quality of something is not measured by multiplying it by the number of people who dig it.

But what I'm really talking about, of course, is that old coincidence. I'm talking about the performer who expects to spend as much money on recording time and engineers and instruments and whatever as is needed to do what he wants to do. No matter how you divide up the wealth of the world, there is not at the present time sufficient time-money-energy on Earth to give every person alive an engineer, a set of musicians, all the instruments he wants and five weeks of time in a well-equipped studio. So anyone who wants all those privileges had better either be a fascist, or a person who is creating for more than a half a dozen people. Because if people will pay for these records that cost so much to make, fine. If you want to spend all that money making the music, and they're willing to spend all that money to listen to it, nothing could be fairer.

But beware the coincidence. I've spent a lot of time in this article trying to get at some of the reasons *why* people are willing to buy what the Stones, the Airplane, and the Beach Boys are trying to do. Why people enjoy the stuff, what they get out of it. What makes it all worthwhile. There are a lot of records I couldn't justify as well. Some of these records cost a lot of money (and I'm not talking about dollars, I'm talking about people, and the time spent by people other than the artist on all the aspects of this process, including earning the "money" to support the process). And some of the artists who made these records are beginning to think they have a god-given right to take up as many people's time as they want in order to do their thing. Jabberwocky!

Beware the baldersnatch, my son. Beware the confusion that comes at the top, that comes from thousands of people waiting for your new album, that comes from record companies standing in line for the right to spend money on you, that comes from fourteen-page magazine articles about how great you are. Remember you are only you, remember that your prime concern should be doing what is most important to you, but that you have a responsibility, a very real responsibility to every person other than yourself who gets involved in the achieving of your personal goals.

That doesn't mean hey sing "White Rabbit" for us, Grace. No, the point is not to think that you have any responsibility to anybody because they've bought your records or whatever they did in the past. The point is to think about the present, think about whether what you're doing is worth whatever is going into it. Because, forgetting the morality of the thing, what happens to our creative artists if nobody buys their new albums and they have to go back to recording in a garage?

Rock music is the first good music in quite a while to

achieve a mass acceptance. It is also one of the few really worthy side-effects of the current state of mass media in the Western world. Because many rock musicians, rock producers, rock etcetera do not appreciate the significance of this, we are in serious danger right now of blowing the whole bit. With the best intentions in the world, the ideal of serving pure art and pure individual creative instinct, we may drive ourselves out of the recording studio and the mass media and back into our garages and audiences of half a dozen friends. If we don't try our damndest to make music that is both of high quality *and* accessible to a fairly widespread audience, we may look pretty silly a year from now complaining that no one pays us any attention.

But I don't want to end on a polemical note. Why, it might cut down the pleasure value of my own creating! And anyway, I think Ray Davies must be the only man ever to have written a song entitled "There's Too Much on My Mind."

"I got no reason to be there, but I imagine it would be some kind of change."

TOP: *David Crosby of The Byrds. Photo by Ken Greenberg.*
BELOW: *Roger McGuinn of The Byrds. Photo by Ken Greenberg.*

2: BLESHING

Sunshine Superman

October 1966

Mild-mannered singer-songwriter Donovan Leitch (better known to the world as Sunshine Superman!) has done a very nice thing for modern-day pop music: he has injected into it a sense of wonder. He looks at the world with a sort of hip innocence, paints his pictures with a dab of irony and a dash of awe, and somehow never neglects the delicate in the decadence around him. He wanders into the past on occasion, but somehow that only serves to reinforce the fact that this is perhaps the most 1966 lp I've ever heard. It has the taste of now.

The album is the first for Donovan in more than a year, and although his style may seem to have changed drastically, it would be more simple and accurate to say that it has improved. If you listen carefully to *Fairytale* (Hickory Records, 1965) after familiarizing yourself with *Sunshine Superman*, you will find that much of the earlier album could have been included in the later without seeming too out of place. "Sunny Goodge Street" and "Summer Day Reflection Song" are musically mature both as compositions and in performance; Donovan employs careful arrangements, imaginative phrasing, and—folkies take note—musical accompaniment beyond simple guitar strumming in both of these 1965 recordings. Some of Donovan's songs are most effective *with* simple guitar strumming, of course; but even when it was hip to be a purist Donovan sensed that it was better to be a maker of music.

So we come eventually to the fact that this album employs musicians and accompaniments galore; but what may be overlooked amid remarks on the sitar, the overdubbing, and the electricity, is the fact that this album has a producer, an excellent one. Mickie Most has succeeded in making it possible for us to hear Donovan's songs much as Don must hear them in his head; clearly, there is a rapport between singer, producer, and accompanists that transcends mere good fortune. Most—or someone; perhaps, as occasionally happens, the performer is largely his own producer—has translated concept into actuality with remarkable grace. And surely a touch of magic enters in—on "Sunshine Superman" one voice starts to sing "forever to be mine" while the lead sings on "you're going to be mine," and the effect, intended or not, is glorious.

For those who like to categorize, the songs fall into approximately ten groups, each as independent and as unexpected as the performer is himself. Donovan reaches out in all directions to give us, his listeners, a sense of what things feel like. In the title song he is all charm, self-confident youth in the morning sunshine, radiating with the feeling that "nothing can stop me." "You're gonna be mine and I know it," he smiles; and if you've ever known springtime you can't fail to understand. It's a teen-age song, with a rock and a lilt and plenty of identifying—but it isn't a sop to the masses, it isn't why-must-I-be-a-teenager-in-love; it's a slice of reality for the youthful among us. Go ahead, roll down the window, rest your elbow in the breeze, turn up the volume a little and sing along with those marvelous verses and their broken rhythm; tap your foot and just appreciate the way all that musical chaos in the accompaniment blends perfectly into a goodtime music that is not in the least Beatles or Lovin' Spoonful or Dylan or anything else that ever was but just pure underivative Donovan, underivative because he's absorbed what needed absorbing and now his music just comes from everywhere, sunshine, moonlight, even—and what could be more 1960's ethnic?—transistor radios. Enjoy.

Following the easy, insistent beat of "Sunshine Superman"

Donovan effortlessly shifts gears to the rhythmless violins and harpsichord of "Legend of a Girl-Child Linda." The early morning time of joy fades into the timelessness of a dream-place, and the transition is perfect. Perhaps it's the sound of that same gentle voice that assures us we haven't been deserted—our guide is simply showing us a different hall in the same gallery of song. "Legend of a Girl-Child Linda" is a pleasant walk through the carefully carved features of a somewhere else, a children's kingdom, a world with the utterly acceptable reality of an identifiable dream. It is not Central Park North—but the story could be told there, to city children gathered in a very now place, heads filled with quiet elsewhere, delicately ornamented with whatever they imagine nature might be. Donovan is here the storyteller; not the child anymore, nor yet good old Uncle Don talking to the kiddies. Rather, his context is one of mature, but child-like, wonder. He is the magician; he knows his tales and shows are but one fifth his own—the other four fifths pro-vided by the listener, the eager child, watching the story-teller's hands and seeing the world he unfolds, but seeing it through his own particular eyes.

And we who aren't quite children, we too take part, weav-ing things our own way with our own visions in mind; and we are captured. On the last verse the singer's voice becomes somehow more stark, and we hear each word: "My sword it lies broken and cast in a lake . . . in the dream I was told that my princess would wake." And suddenly it's not a children's tale at all, except as we are children; it's a song for us, a song of loss and hope, innocence vanished—"cast in a lake"—a feeling of gone forever . . . "In the dream I was told that . . ." and suddenly like cold water we are out of it and seeing it as a dream, and yet sensing how real it was; the princess is remembered as we wake as someone real and loving, and the sense of awakeness and now is less real by far than she was. As Donovan mentions later on ("The Trip"), the world is often quite detached from us; the near-reality of dreams is much more vivid. But there's more here than just loss of dreams—the dream becomes a model for some possible reality . . . "I was told that my princess would wake." One need not analyze all this to feel it; the mark of the artist is that he transmits ideas and feelings directly— neither he nor you need know how or what is transmitted. As long as you don't resist the magician, the spell is cast and Donovan's artistry and relevance come through. As always, enlightenment and entertainment—when both are good— come both in the same package.

"Three Kingfishers" paints its picture all in sound. The tabla—Indian drums—are properly employed; the song does not seem experimental or "east vs. west"ish at all. Donovan is clearly *into* all these sounds—they are his, the feelings he has, his vocal style the common denominator, a needle with which he weaves. And the listener is woven in; as the music continues you become fully a part of it. "Look at the tiny oceans in my hand." You listen, and you see them. It is good that these songs work into each other so well . . . it would be cruel if the cord that is formed were ripped out after each tune. But no, it is all one cord, and even after finishing the album you are tied. It stays with you—once invited in to view the palace you are never thrown out the back door. You live within it, and in the world too. In this way the album is more real than *Revolver*, a frankly experimental lp, a hat shop, try this on for size, and this, and when you've tried on all the hats you leave. *Sunshine Superman* is an experience that continues to affect you; *Revolver* for me is more a one-night stand.

"The Ferris Wheel"—a love song. The amusement park at night; everything is a part of everything and everything is you; I wish you could enjoy it all as I enjoy it all and you. A feeling of oneness. God is love; pantheism. And "Bert's Blues" has such fantastic changes of tempo! Donovan is thinking jazz and singing rock and roll; the cut is the single most unusual musical accomplishment on the album. Yet it's so easy to accept as perfectly natural and expected; it fits. As a halfway point on the lp, it is a wonderful sort of summary-with-introspection—and so simple! "I've been looking for a good gal . . ." "I've been picking up sunshine, drinking down the rain." It is "Sunshine Superman" again, but not quite as exuberant; pausing a moment in the shade, he would still say ". . . you're going to be mine," but he is uncomfortably aware that it hasn't happened yet. He's still waiting. It's a beautiful companion piece to "Sunshine Superman" . . . and to the dream of the princess, and the amusement park vision, and all. Really, the whole lp is one song.

Turn the record over. "Season of the Witch" is the most powerful single track on the album, impossible to listen to without wanting to turn up the volume. The production is excellent, with that great bass line out front, and organ and lead building to a frenzy that makes you almost suspect Donovan's being backed by the Young Rascals (incidentally, it is criminal that nowhere on this lp are the sidemen identified). You can feel the song all through you, and it's all too clear that this *is* the season of the witch: you see Donovan walking down the street with people staring at his hair, people frightened of "beatniks" and uptight about anything different, rabbits running in the ditch, scared and irrational and ready for Salem all over again. And as always Donovan sings no protest and hate but rather: "Sure is strange to see . . ." Judgments are avoided. "The Trip," too, is noncommittal; it's an innocent, honest swirl of visions with heavy irony and mostly just "What goes on? I really want to know." It's a great rolling song, not really about drugs so much as about, well, alienation. Detachment, like. What goes on? And "Guenevere." Donovan says, "All of a sudden I was there, 400 a.d., hiding like a child watching . . ." and I can't really add to that. The song is like walking through very deep snow, which may not seem good but is. "Fat Angel" is an unbelievably funny song about a dealer. Again, Donovan has made his point perfectly. He seems to aim almost blindly, such is his ease—but he never misses. He is a marksman.

Finally, there is "Celeste." The strings are too loud and

"big" for my taste. It's really the only case of poor judgment on the lp—it makes the whole thing come on too strong. But it is definitely the right song, if the wrong performance, to finish the album—again, introspection, this time "Dawn crept in unseen, to find me still awake" (the first words of the lp are, of course, "Sunshine came softly through my window today . . ."). "Would anybody like to try the changes I'm going through?" and "A hidden lie would fortify something that don't exist." So in the end, it is left unsaid; no answer, no "meanings" or "messages," no deception—and no fortification. We have to go it alone. Or almost alone: "a strange young girl" sings her songs for him, as he has for us, and "I would have liked to try the changes that she's going through" . . . and we're back to "I've been looking for a good gal" and "It'll take time, I know it, but in a while, you're gonna be mine and I know it . . ."

Sunshine Superman is an original, moving, perfectly coherent forty-one-minute piece of music.

Buffalo Springfield

January 1967

Let me tell you about popsicle sticks.

To me, a major aspect of rock 1967 is the tightness of the new groups. By tightness, I mean the feeling of wholeness a group projects when they're on stage (or in a recording studio), and I'm thinking of Jefferson Airplane, Moby Grape, the Youngbloods, the Buffalo Springfield, the Doors. An individual, an audience, can react to one of these groups as a unit, can feel a group personality reaching out from the stage. I never listen to Neil Young, the way I might listen to Mike Bloomfield or Jeff Beck, because Neil Young isn't on stage; the Springfield is, and the brilliant things Neil does are an inseparable part of the music the Springfield is making. And Neil's excellent playing isn't just Neil soloing away;

it's Neil reacting to, working with, each Buffalo, and more than that, feeling a certain way about the gig and the song and the run and whatever because of a sense of his place in things, because of his awareness of himself as a Buffalo Springfield. It's a somewhat different feeling from the feeling of being Neil Young, and as a result what he contributes to the group's communication is different from what he'd contribute were he in a different group. Basically, tightness is a matter of finding the right people to work with, people who can form an emotional unit with you as well as a musical unit; a group must have a stable personality, and its personality must relate well to the type of music it works with, for that group to be tight. That doesn't mean everyone has to be best friends—it means the members of the group have to be interacting creatively toward a common goal, a certain sound, for the audience to be able to interact with the group. Conflict—competition—destroy wholeness.

Tightness comes in many flavors. Jefferson Airplane has a dark solidity to its sound, as though each member were a thick black line and the six so close musically that all you see/hear/feel is a deep solid rectangle of sound and personality. The Youngbloods, perhaps the tightest group in the country, are nonetheless four very distinct musicians. You hear four separate things, but you feel one feeling. They are four quarters, working in perfect unity but with a very different oneness from that of a dollar bill. The Buffalo Springfield resemble neither of these groups in their tightness; more distinct as personalities than the Airplane, they are at the same time not as separate as the Youngbloods. If you see the Airplane as a solid rectangle, and the Youngbloods as four separate lines standing together, then the Springfield is/are a crisscross, a popsicle stick construction held together only by the force of each stick on each other stick, a subtle and seemingly delicate wholeness which nonetheless communicates itself extremely powerfully to a receptive audience.

Buffalo Springfield (italicized because that's the name of their album, Atco 33–200) is a lovely, moving experience. You have to be into it, however; chances are you won't even like it on first hearing. All the songs seem to sound alike, and the group sound is quite thin. These are valid criticisms. There are certain samenesses in the Springfield's material, and if you hear them on one of their rare off nights, you'll be quite bored. But what the Springfield do is rise above these samenesses, employing beautiful changes and continually fresh approaches within their particular framework. The more you listen to this album and become familiar with it, the more you'll see in each song. As for the thinness, the production job on this lp is sadly amateurish. The bass is under-recorded, the drums misunderstood, and the guitars tend to tinkle when they want to ring. On stage, the Springfield have a deceptively full sound: they're not as loud or as solid as the Airplane, but because every note each man plays is so perfectly directed—like the popsicle-stick construction—they project a richness and a fullness which is more satisfying than one could possibly imagine. It's a delicate balance, however, and it wasn't achieved in the recording studio. This is partly for production reasons—poor miking, poor mixing, and the wrong studios for the Springfield's sound—but it's also because the group wasn't completely on when they did these sessions. Much more can happen to these songs on a good night than did happen in the studio.

But the album, despite it all, is beautiful. Every track on it will entrance you, at one time or another. "Clancy" will probably be first—both melody and lyric hit very hard, and once the rhythm changes and the phrasing sink in, you're done for. The objectivity of the song is heartbreaking: "Who should be sleeping that's writing this song, wishin' and a-hopin' he weren't so damn wrong?" Straightforwardness—with a sort of implied understatement—is characteristic of the Springfield. Consider the titles of their songs: "Flying on the Ground Is Wrong"; "Sit Down, I Think I Love You"; "Leave." They love to come right out and say it, with a shrug of the shoulders and an innocent look.

But it's not so much innocence as openness; honesty, warmth—these are key words in describing a Buffalo Springfield performance. They present themselves to the people, offering nothing but giving everything. There's love in their music—not the driving, evangelical love of Jefferson Airplane, but a straightforward take-it-or-leave-it love, all yours if you want it and will share in it. If the Springfield leave you cold, it's probably because you want to be left cold; once you get into them, you'll be stunned by their warmth. It's the extraordinary amount of honest emotion conveyed in this lp that makes it exceptional.

"Flying on the Ground" is the song that knocks me out the most just now. It's an unassuming little love song that walks all around the edges of rock's oldest clichés and comes away quietly fresh. "Baby Don't Scold Me" plays with some more recent clichés—mostly Beatles stuff—but still manages to sound 100 percent Buffalo Springfield. The Springfield— no matter what they play—are too much themselves to resemble anyone else; every noise the group makes is riddled with the uniqueness of their personality. This very fact may work against them. At present, the Springfield are an excellent and exciting group, and I would go far from where I am to hear them. But unlike many groups who aren't as good, the Springfield do not strike me as a growing unit, one that will branch out into new fields of musical expression as it finds itself overfamiliar with the field that it's in. Right now the group could release another album in much the same style as the first and still show us new tricks—but another lp after that would be pretty draggy without some major changes. What worries me is that the Springfield are so tight and so spontaneous in what they're doing now that whatever new things they approach they seem to approach in relation to the past. They know what they can do and they do it excellently. But that's not enough; to remain as good as they are, they must get better—they must grow. And while each individual in the group is probably capable of further musical growth, the group as a whole—though it is a brilliantly tight performing unit at present—may not be a tight growing unit as well. I hope I'm wrong about this; meanwhile, it should be remembered that groups, people, must and do change . . . and a fiercely whole musical unit today cannot even count on being together a year from now.

I've purposely avoided discussing the individual Buffaloes; they're all talented—Richie's phrasing is extremely fresh and effective; Dewey is an excellent drummer, comparable to the Hollies' Bobby Elliott; Bruce is surely the secret master of the group; etc.—but to me the group can only be thought of as a unit. I don't want to overlook, however, the songwriting talents of two of the Buffaloes: both Neil and Steve are exceptional quite apart from writing for a specific group—their songs would surely be recorded, though not the same way, if there were no Buffalo S. Steve's "Sit Down, I Think I Love You" is already a West Coast hit in a cover version by the Mojo Men; almost every other song on this lp has the potential to be a single. In few cases could a cover version be better than the Springfield's; but it might well be more commercial. Both Neil and Steve are capable of unusually clever lyrics, song structures and changes that work well, and light, effective melodies. But they never seem to write a song together, though their styles are quite related; it is characteristic of the Springfield that each man does his part, independently, and the parts just fit together.

This album was recorded early last fall; since then the eternal war between Past and Present has broken out anew, this time in open battle on Hollywood's Sunset Strip. Battles tend to beget songs; November's clashes moved Stephen Stills to write the first major topical song since "Hard Rain." "There's something happening here; what it is ain't exactly clear. There's a man with a gun over there, telling me I've got to beware. I think it's time we stop, children, what's that sound? Everybody look what's going down . . ."* The title of the song is perfect: "For What It's Worth." There is no bitter-

* Copyright © 1966 Ten East Springalo, Cotillion Music, Inc.

ness, no dialectic; just description, and a word of unspoken advice: hold back from the battle—look around—we've already won the war.

"For What It's Worth" is the first Buffalo Springfield single to make the charts. It should be at least a million-seller; we owe ourselves that much.

The Byrds' Greatest Hits and Others

August 1967

Sadness is perhaps a word for it, walking down the street with familiar sounds of "Light My Fire" barely audible from an apartment somewhere high above. Timelessness abounds. The song began somewhere centuries back and goes on, in the back of my mind, almost forever. I heard only a few notes, peripheral hearing, an uncertainty that blends the music into all the other background, like the vague smell of a bakery somewhere.

The Doors are good Muzak. Like the Byrds, they are perfect on a highly complex, imperceptible level. Nothing is obvious, nothing protrudes. Everywhere is here, now, current, with no sense of actual immediacy (which would imply consciousness of time) and no knowledge of the definite.

Any greatest hits album is insignificant. By definition it contains nothing unfamiliar; and yet this very fact offers great potential beauty, for a well-made greatest hits lp might then unleash the emotion of familiarity in an artistic context. The Byrds have achieved that goal: always masters of the form, they have now taken the concept of a great hits anthology and created from it an essay into rediscovery.

The opening is masterful. The listener, knowing this is a big hits album, knows he can only expect crass repetition of earlier-recorded material; and yet, staring at that cover, whose beauty has only just begun to work its magic on him, he cannot help but feel that somehow something miraculous is going to take place. Never has there been a Byrds album without a stunning cover, and never has the record itself proved anything less than infinitely greater than its jacket. So you can't quite believe that this will be an exception, and then you hear those beautiful notes that begin the *Tambourine Man* album and the Byrds' careers, and you know that this album too is wonderful, for there is that same joy, that same perfection, but opening a *different* lp . . . and no matter how many times you've played the *Tambourine Man* lp over again, this is the first time since the first time that you have heard that opening as new, as a surprise. Only by somehow recording a new album that again started with "Tambourine Man" could the Byrds restore the listener's virginity, make it possible for you to hear the same thing without ever having heard it before. This is the rediscovery of the world that so many are experiencing through acid, and never before has music captured it so well.

Aretha's "Respect" has got to be played so loud you worry about the neighbors. And twice, like "Tambourine Man." The second time through you begin to notice anticipation, motion as an aspect of vocal stylizing, the temporal nature of music. The song continually catches up and jumps ahead, crescendoes, subsides, and then waits to be played again. The second time through you've already been torn apart, and damned if it doesn't put you back together! "Tambourine Man" rises, and eventually subsides, but with no sense of peak, forcing you to play it over and over again with the curious feeling you've missed something. The song never resolves, never even asks a question, although you think it might, and hence its implications are infinite. The only song I know that is structurally similar to "Tambourine Man," with its peak before it begins and after its end, is "Light My Fire" (which simulates a peak, but a false one, as the singles version of the song proves. Everything really happens off the record).

NEWARK, Aug 17 (AP)—Four representatives of the

South Vietnamese Ministry of Labor visited the Youth Opportunity Center here today to get ideas for manpower training services in their country.

The relationships within any series of well-expressed concepts may be so complex in their implications as to multiply endlessly the concepts involved; which is to say that as you read and reread this sentence in order to make it make sense, you will constantly discover new and different ideas it might contain. Which doesn't mean it *does* contain them, but rather that it generates them; without the sentence you would never have created those ideas. Any confusion as to which sentence I'm referring to is one of the ambiguities that make this statement valid.

The impact of "Tambourine Man" opening the lp is increased and further complicated by the fact that the next song is "I'll Feel a Whole Lot Better," which was also the second song on the *Tambourine Man* album! The effect is somewhat like hearing one very pleasing note for four minutes and fifty seconds. Anticipation of change, of proof that this is *not* the first album but something very different, becomes almost unbearable, until finally the Byrds break into "The Bells of Rhymney," which is likewise on the first side of the first album, but isn't the third song. Such subtlety! Comparable is Aretha Franklin's "You Are My Sunshine," which opens with a brilliant almost *a cappella* vocal that goes on and on unbearably while you clench your teeth and sweat it out waiting for the drums and melody to interrupt. Long after you've decided the damn thing is one long introduction, the real song does begin, and the sense of relief is almost intolerable.

This album is not *The Byrds Greatest Hits* ("It Won't Be Wrong," not included, was a Top 40 hit, whereas "The Chimes of Freedom" was never even released as a single). Nor is it *The Best of the Byrds* (such a collection would certainly not include "Mr. Spaceman"). It is *The Byrds Revisited*, and they actually make the listener experience what Dylan only hinted at in the titles of his fifth and sixth lps.

(Why would you name a three-year-old documentary after ["She's an artist she] don't look back"?)

An aspect of rock creativity often overlooked is programing: the art of transition. Dicken Acraman, legendary discotheque programer who waited four months for Salvation to open and disappeared a week afterward, once followed the Four Tops' "Walk Away Renee" with "Turn, Turn, Turn," in open recognition of the fact that the Byrds are capable of almost any transition at almost any time. On the album "Turn, Turn, Turn" is preceded by "The Bells of Rhymney," as if daring you to think about Pete Seeger. Hearing "Turn, Turn, Turn" on an lp with a Byrds song before and after it is quite an experience; resolving it into "just a song" instead of "their big number one hit" is difficult and extremely satisfying.

An obvious question is, how are you reading this article? Assuming it is written with certain rhythms and concepts of structure, how are you contributing to it? Are you absorbing it all at once? Are you reading it in snatches, and if so, what sort of activity are you mixing into it? (I've watched girls with copies of *Crawdaddy!* bent back in one hand, reading as they crossed against the lights. Other people fall asleep in the middle of a word.) Are you reading this part for the second time?

"The Chimes of Freedom" always wanted to be the last song on a side, so that's all right too.

Greatest hits albums are always regarded as suspect. It's part of the American guilt syndrome: packaging is not considered work (*vid.* Oedipa Maas and Maxwell's Demon) and art without work is invisible. This is crap, of course; the Puritan Ethic; but it is still so strong in this country that it was necessary to invent (and invalidate as art) the concept "put-on" in order to make Andy Warhol famous and yet be able to ignore his genius at the same time. Confronted with this album (and probably this review) the average American scoffs. "It's all done with mirrors!" Yes, it is, and look at that cover again.

Rock criticism is also extremely suspect, as was pointed out to me by none other than David Crosby (he stood up on his hind legs in the Tin Angel and proclaimed, me listening, that "The one thing you absolutely cannot do in this field is intellectualize!"). I think it is understandable and even reasonable for a rock star to want to play God; it was a pretty good *Don't Look Back* parody, and I don't begrudge it. Sandy Pearlman later brought up an interesting point: we write articles about music and art and what's in our minds and stuff, and these performers somehow get the idea we're writing about *them*! This article obviously isn't about the Byrds, and I don't think anybody really thinks it should be.

"Eight Miles High," viewed historically (and a greatest hits album certainly evokes concern with history), was the object of an early confrontation in the war of generations: the Adults banned the record ("You're not allowed to have Strange Experiences, and if you write songs about your Strange Experiences, we're not going to let you listen to them!"). It opens the second side, and these last five songs all reflect the modern version of sadder-but-wiser, which is happier-but-not-so-smart ("I'm younger than that now").

Once again, because of a pun in programing, you are back in an earlier album, and it really is a surprise to hear "Mr. Spaceman" instead of "Hey Joe." Poignant, too, because of the disappointment; and the silly as poignant is a nice achievement.

Go into the bathroom and listen to the Doors. Or listen to the Byrds beside Grand Canyons, stuff like that. The point is to escape space and time: make environment obvious and therefore insignificant. I wrote this paragraph on toilet paper.

But you gotta come back. Listen and look separately, to get the idea, and then integrate them again; beauty is generated by interaction. Closing your eyes and listening to music is primitive, like only being able to hear one instrument at a time. Not that primitive is bad, just that complexity is the life we lead and the more we let go to it the more we ap-

preciate it. Surrender, absorption, boring from within, is
the only real way to possess things. That's what the Man-
churians learned from the Mongols. That's what Haight-
Ashbury is proving to the world (but beware Madison Avenue
bearing gifts . . .).

"Eight Miles High": awe. "Mr. Spaceman": acceptance.
"5D": insight. But any other choices might have been just
as enlightening, for every Byrds song relates to every possible
sequence of Byrds songs, owing to the amount and extent of
implication in each one, and the formal approach that puts
them all in the same approximate plane. I would welcome—
although I don't anticipate—indefinite further permutations
of already existent Byrds material. Perhaps if Columbia
Records would release every track as a stereo single, this
could be achieved.

One of the tortures devised for the "rock critic" is that
he is penalized for not obviously stating the obvious, a torture
in itself. The Byrds are one of the three or four best rock
groups, and everything on this album is—in a rock context—
great.

The transition from "5D" to "Rock 'n' Roll Star" is very
clean and warm, a recognition of the long period of silence
after the release of the former song and the successful
resolution of all the problems that arose before the Byrds
were able to record the latter. And the Byrds' acceptance and
appreciation of themselves as rock 'n' roll stars is historically
fascinating in that it preceded—by just a month or two—
the Beatles' discovery that they really are the Beatles and
that's all right. The Byrds have never doubted that they were
the Byrds, but who the *Byrds* are may still be a mystery.

Which makes "My Back Pages" inevitable. Even Bob
Dylan knew that. *Especially* Bob Dylan.

Significantly, because what's important on this lp is the
transitions, this may be the first album where the little
silences between the songs are more important than the songs
themselves. Consider all the silence between the times you

hear "Light My Fire" or "We Love You" in a week. What kind of music is that silence? Signals? Noise? But definitely created by the songs themselves, beings that define all the nothingness. "And if he left off dreaming about you, where do you suppose you'd be?"

For a last sentence, anything with "context" in it is okay.

Bob Dylan. Photo by Elliott Landy.

3: TOM PAINE HIMSELF

Understanding Dylan

July 1966

Perhaps the favorite indoor sport in America today is discussing, worshiping, disparaging, and above all interpreting Bob Dylan. According to legend, young Zimmerman came out of the west, grabbed a guitar, changed his name and decided to be Woody Guthrie. Five years later he had somehow become Elvis Presley (or maybe William Shakespeare); he had sold out, plugged in his feet, and was rumored to live in a state of perpetual high (achieved by smoking rolled-up pages of *Newsweek* magazine). Today, we stand on the eve of his first published book (*Tarantula*) and the morning after his most recent and fully realized lp (*Blonde on Blonde*), and there is but one question remaining to fog our freshly minted minds: what in hell is really going on here?

Who is Bob Dylan, and—this is the question that is most incessantly asked—what is he really trying to say? These are not, as such, answerable questions; but maybe by exploring them we can come to a greater understanding of the man and his songs. It is as an approach to understanding that I offer you this essay.

Everyone knows that Dylan came east from the North Country in 1960, hung around the Village, and finally got a start as a folksinger. If you're interested in biographical information, I recommend a book with the ridiculous title of *Folk-Rock: The Bob Dylan Story*. The authors' attempts at interpretations of songs are clumsy, but the factual portion of the book is surprisingly reasonable (there is no such word as "accurate"). The book perpetuates a few myths, of

59

course (for instance, the name Dylan actually comes from an uncle of Bob's and *not* from Dylan Thomas); and it has its stylistic stumblings. But for just plain (irrelevant) biographical info, the book is worth your 50 cents.

There are a few things about Dylan's past that *are* relevant to understanding his work (or to not misunderstanding it), however, and these appear to be little known. His roots are deep in country music and blues: he lists Percy Mayfield and Charlie Rich among the musicians he admires most. But he did not start out as a "folksinger," not in the currently accepted sense. From the very beginning his desire was to make it in the field of rock and roll.

In 1960, however, rock and roll was not an open field. The songs were written in one part of town, then sent down to the recording companies in another part of town where house artists recorded them, backed by the usual house bands. A country kid like Dylan didn't stand a chance of getting into rock and roll, and it did not take him long to find that out. The only way he could get anyone to listen to him—and the only way he could keep himself alive—was to start playing the coffeehouses. This got him a recording contract and an interested audience, as well as a reputation as a folksinger, and it was one of the luckiest things that ever happened to him. First of all, it put him under pressure to produce; and nothing better can happen to any young writer. Secondly, it made him discipline his songwriting, and though he may have resented it at the time, it was this forced focusing of his talents that made them emerge. You have to learn some rules before you can break them.

But it was inevitable that "folk music" would only be a temporary harbor. "Everybody knows that I'm not a folk singer," he says; and, call him what you will, there is no question that by the time *Another Side of Bob Dylan* appeared he was no longer thinking his songs in terms of simple guitar accompaniments (to a certain extent, he never had been). He was straining at the bit of folk music's accepted patterns, and fearing, perhaps rightly so, that no one was interested in what he wanted to say any more. But then "Tambourine Man" caught on, and people began responding to him as a man and not as a politician. The light was green: he'd been working very hard on a very important song, and he decided he was going to sing it the way he heard it. That was "Like a Rolling Stone," and its success meant that from now on he could do a song any way he wanted. "I knew how it had to be done," he says; "I went out of my way to get the people to record it with me."

It was a breakthrough. He was into the "rock and roll field" for real now, but of course he is no more a rock and roll singer than a folksinger. He is simply an artist able to create in the medium that for him is most free.

I have gone into this background only because there continues to be so much useless misunderstanding, so much talk about "folk-rock," so much discussion of "the old Dylan" and "the new Dylan." Until you, as a listener, can hear *music* instead of categories, you cannot appreciate what you are hearing. As long as people persist in believing that Dylan would be playing his new songs on a folk guitar instead of with a band, except that recording with a band brings him more money, they will fail to realize that he is a creator, not a puppet, and a creator who has reached musical maturity. Dylan is doing his songs now the way he always wanted to do them. He is a bard who has found his form, no more, no less; and if you're interested in what he's saying, you must listen to him on his own terms.

It is my personal belief that it is not the artist but his work that is important; therefore, I hesitate to go too deeply into the question of *who* Bob Dylan is. Owl and Churchy once had a fantastic fight over whether a certain phrase actually fell from the lips of Mr. Twain, or Mr. Clemens. And someone has pointed out that nobody knows if the *Odyssey* was written by Homer or by another early Greek poet of the same name. Perhaps I don't make myself clear. I only want to point out that if we found out tomorrow that Bob Dylan was a 64-year-old woman who'd changed her sex, and a proven Communist agent, we might be surprised, but the words to "Mr. Tambourine Man" would not change in the slightest. It would still be the same song.

I will say, to dispel any doubts, that Mr. Dylan is not a 64-year-old woman or an agent of anything. I met him in Philadelphia last winter; he is a friendly and straightforward young man, interested in what others are saying and doing, and quite willing to talk openly about himself. He is pleased with his success; he wanted it, he worked for it honestly, and he's achieved it. We talked about the critics, and he says he resents people who don't know what's going on and pretend they do. He named some names; it is my fervid hope that when this article is finished, and read, my name will not be added to the list.

It is difficult to be a critic; people expect you to *explain* things. That's all right if you don't know what's going on . . . you can make up almost any clever-sounding explanation, and people will believe you. But if you do understand a poem, or a song, if it is important to you, then chances are you also understand that you're destroying it if you try to translate it into one or two prose sentences in order to tell the guy next door "what it means." If you could say everything that Dylan says in any one of his songs in a sentence or two, then there would have been no point in writing the songs. The sensitive critic must act as a guide, not paraphrasing the songs but trying to show people how to appreciate them.

One problem is that a lot of people don't give a damn about the songs. What interests them is whether Joan Baez is "Queen Jane," or whether or not Dylan dedicated "Tambourine Man" to the local dope peddler. These people, viewed objectively, are a fairly objectionable lot; but the truth is that all of us act like peeping toms now and then. Dylan himself pointed this out in a poem on the back of *Another Side*. He wanders into a mob, watching a man about to jump off the Brooklyn Bridge; "I couldn't stay an look at him/because i suddenly realized that/deep in my heart/i really wanted/t see him jump." It is a hard thing to admit that we are potential members of the mob; but if you admit it, you can fight it—you can ignore your curiosity about Dylan's personal life and thoughts, and appreciate his generosity in offering you as much as he has by giving you his poems, his songs. In the end you can know Bob Dylan much better than you know your next door neighbor, because of what he shows you in his songs; but first you have to listen to his songs, and stop treating him as though he lived next door.

Another problem, and in a way a much more serious one, is the widespread desire to "find out" what Dylan's trying to say instead of listening to what he is saying. According to him: "I've stopped composing and singing anything that has either a reason to be written or a motive to be sung. . . . The word 'message' strikes me as having a hernia-like sound." But people go right on looking for the "message" in everything Dylan writes, as though he were Aesop telling fables. Not being able to hear something, because you're too busy listening for the message, is a particularly American malady. There's a tragic lack of freedom in being unable to respond to things because you've been trained to await the commercial and conditioned to listen for the bell.

Take a look at a great painting, or a Polaroid snapshot. Does it have a message? A song is a picture. You see it; more accurately, you see it, taste it, feel it . . . Telling a guy to listen to a song is like giving him a dime for the roller coaster. It's an experience. A song is an experience. The guy who writes the song and the guy who sings it each feel something; the idea is to get you to feel the same thing, or something like it. And you can feel it *without knowing what it is*.

For example: you're a sixth grader, and your teacher reads

you Robert Frost's "Stopping by the Woods on a Snowy Evening." The poem sounds nice; the words are perhaps mysterious, but still powerful and appealing. You don't know what the poem "means," but you get this feeling; the idea of having "miles to go before I sleep" is a pretty simple one, and it means a lot to you. The poet has reached you; he has successfully passed on the feeling he has, and now you have it too.

Years later you read the poem again, and suddenly it seems crystal clear that the poem is about death, and the desire for it. That never occurred to you as a sixth grader, of course; does that mean you originally misunderstood the poem? Not necessarily. Your teacher could say "We want the peace death offers, but we have responsibilities, we are not free to die"; but it wouldn't give you anything. It's a sentence, a platitude. You don't even believe it unless you already know it's true. What the poet does is something different: walking through the woods, he gets a feeling that is similar to the idea your teacher offered you in a sentence. But he does not want to tell you what he believes; that has nothing to do with you. Instead, he tries to make you feel what he feels, and if he succeeds, it makes no difference whether you understand the feeling or not. It is now a part of your experience. And whether you react to the poem as a twelve-year-old, or an English professor, it is the feeling you get that is important. Understanding is feeling . . . the ability to explain means nothing at all.

The way to "understand" Dylan is to listen to him. Listen carefully; listen to one song at a time, perhaps playing it over and over to let it sink in. Try to see what he's seeing— a song like "Visions of Johanna" or "Sad-Eyed Lady of the Lowlands" (or almost any of his more recent songs) is full of pictures, moods, images: persons, places and things. "Inside the museums," he sings, "infinity goes up on trial." It doesn't *mean* anything; but you know what a museum feels like to you, and you can see the insides of one, the particular way people look at things in a museum, the atmosphere, the sort of things that are found there. And you have your image of a trial, of a courtroom: perhaps you don't try to picture a lazy-eight infinity stepping up to the witness chair, but there's a solemnity about a trial, easily associable with the image of a museum. And see how easily the feeling of infinity slips into your museum picture, endless corridors and hall-ways and rooms, a certain duskiness, and perhaps the trial to you becomes the displaying of infinity on the very walls of the museum, like the bones of an old fish, or maybe the fact that museums do have things that are old in them ties in somehow . . . there's no *explanation*, because the line (from "Visions of Johanna," by the way) *is* what it is, but cer-tainly the line, the image, can turn into something living in-side your mind. You simply have to be receptive . . . and of course it is a prerequisite that you live in a world not too unlike Dylan's, that you be aware of museums and court-rooms in a way not too far different from the way he is, that you be able to appreciate the images by having a similar cultural background. It is not necessary that you understand mid-century America and the world of its youth in order to understand Dylan; but you do have to be a part of those worlds, or the songs will lose all relevance. This is true of most literature, in a way; and of course Dylan has his ele-ments of universality as well as his pictures of the specific.

I *could* explain, I suppose. I could say that "Memphis Blues Again" is about displacement, and tell you why Dylan would think of a senator as "showing everyone his gun." But the truth is, that wouldn't give you anything. If you can't feel it, you can't get anything out of it; you can sneer and say "It's commercialism" or "It's about drugs, and I'm above it," but not only are you dead wrong, you're irrelevant.

In many ways, understanding Dylan has a lot to do with understanding yourself. For example, I can listen to "Sad-Eyed Lady of the Lowlands" and really feel what the song is about, appreciate it; but I have no idea why "a warehouse eyes my

Arabian drums" or what precise relevance that has. Yet it does make me feel something; the attempt to communicate is successful, and somehow the refrain "Now a warehouse eyes my Arabian drums" has a very real relevance to me and my understanding of the song. So it isn't fair to ask Dylan what the phrase means, or rather, why it works; the person I really have to ask is the person it works on—me. And *I* don't know why it works—i.e., I can't explain it. This only means I don't understand me; I do understand Dylan— that is, I appreciate the song as fully as I believe is possible. It's the example of the sixth grader and Robert Frost all over again.

If you really want to understand Dylan, there are perhaps a few things you can do. Read the poems on the backs of his records; read his book when it comes out; read the brilliant interview that appeared in last April's *Playboy*. But above all listen to his albums; listen carefully, and openly, and you will see a world unfold before you. And if you can't see his songs by listening to them, then I'm afraid that all the explaining in the world will only sink you that much deeper in your sand trap.

We have established, I hope, that art is not interpreted but experienced (whether or not Dylan's work is art is not a question I'm interested in debating at the moment. I believe it is; if you don't, you probably shouldn't have read this far). With that in mind, let's take a cursory look at *Blonde on Blonde,* an excellent album which everyone with any admiration for the work of Bob Dylan should rush out and buy at once.

Two things stand out: the uniform high quality of the songs (in the past Dylan's lps have usually, in my opinion, been quite uneven) chosen for this extralong lp; and the wonderful, wonderful accompaniments. Not only is Dylan's present band, including himself on harmonica, easily the best backup band in the country, but they appear able to read his mind. On this album, they almost inevitably do the right thing at the right time; they do perfect justice to each of his songs, and that is by no means a minor accomplishment. *Blonde on Blonde* is in many ways—the quality of the sound, the decisions as to what goes where in what order, the mixing of the tracks, the timing, etc.—one of the best-produced records I've ever heard, and producer Bob Johnston deserves immortality at least. Certainly, Dylan's songs have never been better presented.

And they really are fine songs. It's hard to pick a favorite; I think mine is "Memphis Blues Again," a chain of anecdotes bound together by an evocative chorus ("Oh, Mama, can this really be the end, To be stuck inside of Mobile with the Memphis blues again?"). Dylan relates specific episodes and emotions in his offhand impressionistic manner, somehow making the universal specific and then making it universal again in that oh-so-accurate refrain. The arrangement is truly beautiful; never have I heard the organ played so effectively (Al Kooper, take a bow).

"I Want You" is a delightful song. The melody is attractive and very catchy; Dylan's voice is more versatile than ever; and the more I listen to the musicians backing him up the more impressed I become. They can't be praised enough. The song is lighthearted, but fantastically honest; perhaps what is most striking about it is its inherent innocence. Dylan has a remarkably healthy attitude toward sex, and he makes our society look sick by comparison (it is). Not that he's trying to put down anybody else's values—he simply says what he feels, and he manages to make desire charming in doing so. That is so noble an achievement that I can forgive him the pun about the "queen of spades" (besides, the way he says, "I did it . . . because time is on his side" is worth the price of the album).

"Obviously Five Believers" is the only authentic rock and roll song on the record, and it reflects Dylan's admiration of the early rock and rollers. Chuck Berry and Larry Williams are clear influences. "I'd tell you what it means if I just didn't have to try so hard," sings Bob. It's a joyous song; harp, guitar, vocal, and lyrics are all groovy enough to practically unseat Presley retroactively.

"Rainy Day Women #'s 12 & 35" (the uncut original) is brilliant in its simplicity: in a way, it's Dylan's answer to the uptight cats who are searching for messages. This one has a message, and it couldn't be clearer, or more outrageously true. *Time* magazine is just too damn stoned to appreciate it.

I could go on and on, but I'm trying hard not to. The album is notable for its sense of humor ("Leopard Skin Pillbox Hat" and "Pledging My Time" and much else), its pervading, gentle irony (in "4th Time Around," for example), its general lack of bitterness, and above all its fantastic sensitivity ("Sad-Eyed Lady of the Lowlands" should become a classic; and incidentally, whoever decided it would sound best alone on a side, instead of with songs before it and after it, deserves a medal for good taste).

"(Sooner or Later) One of Us Must Know" is another favorite of mine: in its simplicity it packs a punch that a more complex song would often pull. "Visions of Johanna" is rich but carefully subdued ("The country music station plays soft but there's nothing really nothing to turn off" . . . I love that); Dylan's world, which in *Highway 61* seemed to be bubbling over the edges of its cauldron, now seems very much in his control. Helplessness is still the prevalent emotion ("Honey, why are you so hard"), but chaos has been relegated to the periphery. Love (and sex, love's half-sister) are all-important, and love, as everyone knows, has a certain sense of order about it, rhyme if not reason. No one has to ask (I hope) what "I Want You" is about, or "Absolutely Sweet Marie." Or "Just Like a Woman," which I want to cut out of the album and mail to everybody. The songs are still a swirl of imagery, but it is a gentler, less cyclonic swirl; more like autumn leaves. The nightmares are receding.

Blonde on Blonde is a cache of emotion, a well-handled package of excellent music and better poetry, blended and meshed and ready to become a part of your reality. Here is a man who will speak to you, a 1960's bard with electric lyre and color slides, a truthful man with X-ray eyes you can look through if you want. All you have to do is listen.

The Period of Silence

August 1967

As I write this—August 1967—Bob Dylan has been silent for more than a year. It's been a curious calm. Between *Highway 61 Revisited* and *Blonde on Blonde* was a gap of some ten months—but a gap broken up with the release of several 45's of exciting new material, a winter concert tour, a fascinating interview in *Playboy,* and finally the cheerful, triumphant "Rainy Day Women"—"Everybody must get stoned."

1967 has offered no such relief. Dylan suffered severe damage—three broken vertebrae—in a motorcycle accident in August 1966, and retired from public view. All concerts were canceled—first till January, then March, then—perhaps —forever. *Tarantula,* Dylan's much-promoted first book, never appeared. TV specials scheduled for ABC-TV and the BBC in Britain were canceled amid bad will and lawsuits. MGM announced it had signed Dylan, discovered it hadn't, and prudently shut up; and meanwhile Columbia issued a greatest hits lp, just to be on the safe side. And still no sign of a new recording.

And why should we be so concerned? It has been Dylan's unwilling, unfortunate fate to be somehow responsible to the world for every move he makes. A year is not a long time in an artist's life—some writers have been silent for twenty— and surely a man deserves as much time to do his work in private, and as much time to simply relax, as he can possibly obtain. This is the least any of us might ask; and yet if Dylan retreats he is considered not hardworking but somehow cowardly, unwilling to show the world his rough drafts, unwilling to work and create in a fishbowl, mounted on a pedestal in Times Square. Dylan is our most-loved living poet, and the public that has embraced him now believe they possess him—he must behave according to their will.

They hold him responsible for the passage of time; sometimes he must think that. At Newport, Forest Hills, 1965, his fans dictated what he could and could not play, and with what instrument! The "folk music boom"—actually an early stage of modern pop music and not deserving of the name folk at all—progressed properly into a freer, more complex form of creative music; and *Sing Out* and the mad dogs of the "folk boom" led a witch hunt against the man most prominently identified with the changes music was undergoing. Bob Dylan and his electric guitar were held responsible for the plight of every ambitious "folk" singer who found himself out of fashion. "Dylan did it!" they screamed. "You got a lot of nerve . . ." answered Bob, but he was deeply hurt. He'd been concerned with his music, his poems—he'd never tried to carry the world on his shoulders.

But the world wants to be on his shoulders. We expect our artists to take care of us. Or so it has been; but maybe, just perhaps, this last year of silence has been a time of learning, not just for Dylan but for his fans. Deprived of a new lp, we return to what he's done before . . . at some point *Highway 61* or *Another Side of* or *The Times They Are A-Changin'* has crept back on the phonograph, and the songs have been heard a new way. "It ain't me babe . . . no, no, no, it ain't me babe; it ain't me you're lookin' for." Does the girl who first heard that at nineteen, a champion of Peace, defender of the Negro, and veteran of her first traumatic freshman affair, now discover the song at twenty-two? It doesn't seem as sad, perhaps; she's come and gone and discovered that sometimes it just ain't him, or it just ain't you, and there's nothing anyone can do about it; she suspects that maybe the words mean a little less than she thought they did, but maybe they evoke a little more . . . And the young glue-sniffer who so proudly uncovered "Tambourine Man" as a song about a dealer now hears it again, and the thought strikes him that if he thought the word "dealer" was supposed to have risqué connotations, or if he thought the song incomprehensible without its "secret meaning," then he was a silly child and as wrong as night is dark. For now he listens to Dylan's song and hears the singing joy, feels it all on the surface with no need of a secret decoder, realizes that whether Mr. Tambourine Man is a connection or a Cub Scout den mother, or just a close close friend, what counts is the feeling, the surrender and the joy, the sense of wonder and discovery, and the bright jingle-jangle morning all around you.

Dylan has been silent. But songs are never silent—they speak, long after they've been spoken. Dylan's songs do not decay in time; rather, time flows over them, enriches them, filling in the little cracks we did not understand. "My Back Pages"; "Baby Blue"; "One Too Many Mornings"—these songs have meaning now, and always will. Dylan owes us nothing. We owe him already more than we can give.

God Bless America

January 1968

So stop what you're doing, and hello to *John Wesley Harding*. The medium is the messenger, and wicked is as wicked does, anyway. Don't ask me nothin' about nothin'. Bob Dylan welcomes us all back to the center ring, with many pithy wisdoms which we can take at surface value, surface value at a depth of ten feet, surface value at a depth of twenty feet, and on. "Nothing is revealed." Which is not to imply that the whole album may be unfathomable: at least the soundings are good. But why all these nautical jokes?

I don't know what it means not to understand. It's really an intransitive verb. Transitive stuff like "interpret" might hang you up with all sorts of doubts about will and the ability to choose and all, but there's no freedom involved in understanding. You've gone and done it even if you chose not to. And since you and I never quite see through the same eyeballs anyway, what do you care who understands which? We'll all grow old together.

But I know what you mean. When you're out on the balcony saying run come see the lovely sunset and I look out commenting that's a three-winged caterpillar and anyway the woods are full of them, there *is* a sense of communications loss which undermines togetherness. A drag. And people who *know* they don't perceive the same whatever as the rest of us generally have trouble with the feds. Crazy is not putting on a good enough act. Too many caterpillars, and they take you away.

So let's run *John Wesley Harding* through the analysis mill and see if we can grind it down to oatmeal wretched enough to be universally palatable. All gazing at the same Waterloo Sunset. And how come nobody ever talks about Madison Avenue any more? Like, John Wesley Hardin at fifteen killed a nigger for being uppity, and kept up that kind of bullshit until 1878, when, foolish move or no, he got stuck in jail for sixteen years, missing his twenty-sixth through forty-first birthdays and the inaugurations of Grover Cleveland.

Bob Dylan is nobody's fool. He knows about John Wesley Hardin. Don't underestimate him, and he'll scratch your back too. But dear landlord, this is a mighty intentional record. Intentional and accessible, and that's a tricky combination. Because if Dylan really knows how accessible it is, then maybe he's playing around with the ways that we're going to access it. Wheels within wheels, generating spheres if you're clever enough to tilt them, and at this point there's a lot of control being exercised over the unpredictable. Said Frankie Lee with a smile.

So the way you react might be part of the STOP PRESS! STOP PRESS! 3&77##seven minutes* *Stand By*. PARANOID X, with a message from your sponsor:

"Let us not talk falsely now, the hour is getting late." Mr. Parks thought it "very nice" of Mr. Dylan to say this, and we all concurred. Trina noticed "two riders were approaching, the wind began to howl," and in our several ways we tried to remember how the song had begun.

THERE MUST BE SOME WAY OUT OF HERE . . . THERE MUST BE SOME WAY OUT OF HERE . . .

"All along the watchtower . . ." and it somehow bothered me that the line only appeared once in the song. It had seemed like twice, but . . . And, kindly! The Thief he *kindly* said! Certainly was seeming Meaningful . . .

"There are many here among us who feel that life is but a joke." Well, we laughed and laughed.

But if Bob Dylan is nice enough to empathize with Mick Jagger (". . . no relief") then thieves might be all right too, and you can feel sorry for a joker with claustrophobia. Naturally if you start in the middle it seems like you need to look for a way out, and all; no reason to get excited, that's okay, only, now that we've done that, well, the hour is getting late . . .

And it's a real feeling of friendship when he can say, let us not talk falsely now; Mr. Parks appreciates that sort of thing, and maybe we all wouldn't mind being polite. If the hour really was getting late, and the thief was sympathetic to our occasional panic.

But this isn't "the hour that the ship comes in." And even though it sounds like Bob Dylan's 115th dream, it's not the same. There's some business to take care of, folks, and Dylan can make the song more pleasant for you by starting in the middle, but in the end you've got to start at the beginning, if you know what I mean. Just a joke. But let us not talk falsely now . . .

There must be some way out of here. There must be some way out of here.*

* Lyrics to "All Along the Watchtower" Copyright © 1968 by Dwarf Music.

End of flash. But where does this leave *The Notorious Byrd Brothers*? Well, for one thing, it's obviously the same Bob Dylan, even though he's hard to find on the cover, and curiously enough it's the exact same Byrds even if there's two in the bush. And mainly you have this incredible self-awareness, the artist knowing what he wants to do, and why, and just churning it out, just like any old accepted creative type. In addition to which you have the good old America of science fiction and Tom Paine; and the Byrds have completely let go to bossa nova and square dance and eight miles high the same way Dylan has delightfully done a total Percy Mayfield, Sonny Boy Williamson Live in London (at the Crawdaddy Club!) with the Yardbirds, Eric von Schmidt, Geoff Muldaur, everything you could possibly want if we'd finally gotten around to just digging music. Sort of like Love doing their movie music album, and Van Dyke Parks just being accepted on all fronts. We really are set free.

And on a straight sociological level, that's important. When Dylan started playing Those Instruments, back in the Forest Hills/Newport days, he really did make it possible for a lot of serious and also okay music listeners to begin making that tough transition into rock. And now the general importance of listening to a Dylan album, even if it does sound like some half-country half-blues guy with clever old Nashville cats helping him along, some guy who might in fact just be on the verge of inventing rock and roll in say 1954, even if it sounds like all that nice ethnic music that everyone can dig but no one can really get into, well, you've *got to* get into it because it's a Dylan album. And now I can start giving all my rock friends Percy Mayfield records. Because you can only listen to music openly and comfortably if you *want to* listen to it; and you only used to want to listen to it if it was Folk Ethnic, but it turned out then that you wanted to also if it was Bob Dylan, so you got stuck finding out about rock. And now you wouldn't want to listen to Sonny

Boy Williamson, though you might say "that's nice" if I
played you a little, but since nothing could be more exciting
than a new Dylan album, why, here you are getting into it.
Good old rock, expanding our minds, opening us up to the
world, making us comfortable with and therefore able to
appreciate more and more subtle, good stuff. Rock, the
friendly music. Bob Dylan, frontier scout. Sociologists, take
note.

And it all has to do with contexts. Like everyone else,
I'm sure you have flashed one way or another on the realization that all things are related to all other things. That thing
A, transcendental meditation, can always be related to thing
B, spider crabs, if you do it step by step: APE ARE ARM
AIM DIM DIN DEN MEN MAN. So it stands to reason
that folksong A and rock-song B are always related, can
always be made to share *some* sort of fairly specific category.
There are more categories, therefore, than there are songs;
so why categorically dislike things? To say (even to yourself) I only really enjoy classical music is like saying, I only
enjoy songs whose second verses begin with the letter *m*.
To have an open mind is to be unrestricted by the arbitrary,
at least some of the time. Without such occasional indiscriminate behavior, how could sunsets and caterpillars be
made to coexist? How would we talk to each other?

And you wanted to read about Bob Dylan. A friend of
mine confided that he felt considerable tension in listening to
this album, and I think I can understand why. I get the
same feeling. It has to do with everything on this album's
being at least relatively accessible, and at the same time so
damn intentional; so any time you happen to say to yourself,
"I wonder why he did that," you really feel obliged to work
at figuring it out. 'Cause you know he did it on purpose.
Earlier Dylan records seemed hard to listen to, at first, because so much was baffling; but we quickly overcame that
by not getting up tight about what we didn't understand—
instead, just listening and enjoying what we felt. This new

album, which could be called merely a new arrangement of all those earlier names and prepositions, is so easy to just listen to that you can't help absorbing all the words and getting involved in their implications; and pretty soon you're all tense wondering what in hell he meant by that? When few things are baffling they become all-important.

Which is, I think, what Paranoid X was trying to tell us. "All Along the Watchtower"—a nice song. But certain minor questions arise. Why does it end "two riders were approaching . . ."? Why does the phrase "all along the watchtower" seem somehow out of place? Why is "There must be some way out of here" so incredibly successfully claustrophobic? Why are we drawn to "so let us not talk falsely now, the hour is getting late"? On an lp that is so very comprehensible on an objective level, you can't help getting involved in these subjective questions. And that's why I say Dylan-as-artist is even playing around with our personal reactions to the stuff.

Because, without these subjective questions, I would never have discovered the most delightful aspect of the song. Its ends have been twisted, and taped together. In another universe, Dylan would begin: "All along the watchtower, princes kept the view . . . Two riders were approaching, the wind began to howl." The second and third verses would then be conversation between the two riders, the Joker and the Thief; and "Let us not talk falsely now" would close the song with comfort.

But only in this universe, with the song dissatisfying because the end seems to be in the middle of things, and the beginning stuck in there on the third verse, only in this world can the real claustrophobia of the Joker come through to us all. Because indeed, "There must be some way out of here"— what more natural reaction, caught on a moebius strip?

When people ask me why I get scared on trips, I can point to this song.

And of course it has to do with Time. As more and more people get off the trolley ride, fewer and fewer are aware of

9 to 5, and SMTWTFS. And people's ages. And which album came first. The existence of the jet doesn't mean you can be everywhere at once, but it certainly allows you to think of your life in space as more than a point on a line. And the more we read Borges and Pynchon and listen to rock, the more we ignore the supposed directionality of Time. After months and years, lovers continue to say "hello." Time only takes place in our minds . . . and as we realize this, our minds become more than one-dimensional. We don't have to always hear "Like a Rolling Stone" as after "Subterranean Homesick Blues" and prior to *Blonde on Blonde*. We retain that feeling of progress, but discard the "future" and "the past."

And the music makes it seem so easy. It's all incredible, probably the best electric bass-playing on record and truly brilliant, virtuoso work by the drums and steel guitar. Dylan's voice on this album is so good, is put to such excellent use, that the stubbornest of doubters will be knocked out more than once. His piano makes "Dear Landlord" the work of one of the world's finest blues combos. And the guitar and harmonica provide that persistent link with the other albums, droning along and shaping everything in Dylan's own image. Jes' fine. The whole album offers this sense of shelter, of quietness and ease and protection with everything else that exists in the world ever-so-gently implied in the knotty wood of the cabin walls. "Down Along the Cove" is just about as nice as music can be.

I think I copped out. Looking back on this discussion, I don't think I ran *John Wesley Harding* through the analysis mill at all; I seem to have circled it warily, poking at a theme here or there but never really pouncing on the beast. I haven't told you why this strikes me as the most American record I've ever heard; I haven't described these songs as being Dylan's usual stuff but in different focus; I haven't even gotten onto such grand topics as The Folk Process in Woodstock and Hibbing, or Will the Real John Wesley Hardin Please Stand Up?

But what the hell. I just might be doing it on purpose. Without the deceptions of Time, who really knows the shortest possible distance between two points, and anyway how would it be possible for me to bring up a subject that *didn't* relate to Bob Dylan? If you gaze long enough to see *both* caterpillars and sunsets, whole universes might open up; which is, I think . . .

Enough of that. In *Lot 49* is a lawyer, a child actor turned lawyer whose friend the lawyer-turned-actor is playing the part of him in a movie; and, as Metzger, the lawyer, points out, to portray the role properly the actor must act like a lawyer, who, after all, becomes an actor in the courtroom in front of the judge, and in this case was in fact an actor previously . . . "The film is in an air-conditioned vault at one of the Hollywood studios, light can't fatigue it, it can be repeated endlessly."

Pynchon calls this the "extended capacity for convolution" (or anyway Metzger does) (or I just did); Dylan says, "There must be some way out of here," and . . .

No, come to think of it, the Joker said it . . .

"You can be in my dream if I can be in yours; *I* said that . . ."

So the way you react might be part of the

```
┌─────────────────────────┐
│ this  is  the  way      │
│       out of here ──────▶│
└─────────────────────────┘
```

Bob Weir of The Grateful Dead.
Photo by David Flooke.

4: WHAT WENT ON

June 1967

Johann Sebastian Bach's latest single is out, and like his "Lover's Concerto" of a few years back, it's an easy million-seller. This one is called "A Whiter Shade of Pale": lyrics by Keith Reid, music adapted from the Bach cantata "Sleepers Awake." Procol Harum recorded the song, and it's the fastest-selling record in British Decca's history; equally unprecedented success has been achieved in France, Holland, Belgium, and Switzerland. And by the time you read this, "Pale" should be at least number one in the U.S. with total international sales of about three million. Not bad for a song recorded in one take by a group less than three months old. : : : And if you like that Bach-rock stuff, I recommend *Jazz Guitar Bach* (Nonesuch 71069), a collection of Bach pieces played wonderfully on electric guitar by Andre Benichou and his Well-Tempered Three. Very fine.

Jeff Beck and Mike Bloomfield really started something. Lead guitarists are deserting their groups left and right; John Simmons has joined the Daily Flash (a fine group who, like so many before them, are shriveling on the Greene & Stone vine), replacing Doug Hastings who has joined the Buffalo Springfield in place of Neil Young, who was last seen heading towards England [now back in the Springfield]. The most recent Buffalo Springfield release, "Bluebird"/"Mr. Soul," features instrumental tracks recorded by Greene & Stone in Los Angeles while the Springfield were in New York. The vocals and Neil's overdubbed lead guitar were added later; the resulting mess is an insult to a fine group and some fine material. : : : Meanwhile, Zal Yanovsky has left the Lovin'

Spoonful ("I was getting bored") to pursue a solo career. His replacement is Jerry Yester, formerly of the Modern Folk Quartet.

"Respect" (Aretha Franklin) and "Sweet Soul Music" (Arthur Conley), both songs written by Otis Redding, recently made #1 and #2 on the charts, respectively; but Otis himself has never had a top twenty record in the pop market. : : : Mick Jagger and Keith Richards have been convicted in England of possession of narcotics (meth and hash)—Mick received a three-month sentence, Keith a full year. They're appealing the convictions; meanwhile, Brian Jones is being tried on similar charges. This means that you're unlikely to see the Stones in the U.S. any more, even after they're out of jail. (Donovan has been absent from the States for the same reason.) It may also mean no new album (*Flowers* is made up of leftovers from previous lps) for quite a while . . .

Good news: Carl Wilson has been cleared of draft-dodging charges against him; he still has not achieved the C.O. status he deserves, however. It is unclear at this point when the Beach Boys will release *Smile,* or any new album; there are too many conflicting reports. Let's hope that Brian will not fall into the trap of becoming so enamored of perfection that he produces nothing rather than produce the imperfect (even though he may be six times better now, the work he did last December is more deserving of release than 99.44% of what's available by anybody else).

The Left Banke have reunited with Mike Brown at the helm. : : : "Donovan's Colours," by George Washington Brown (and Van Dyke Parks) is now available on a Warner Brothers 45. It's two years ahead of its time, and required listening for *Crawdaddy!* people. : : : The Walker Brothers have split up and are pursuing solo careers. : : : Premature Award for Liner Notes of the Year goes to Andy Wickham for the Brass Ring *Disadvantages* lp (not much inside the jacket, but wow!). : : : : Love are shifting personnel as usual, and have gone back into the studios to record a new album.

Keep a Straight Face Department (from the *New Musical Express*): "Nancy Sinatra has been signed to co-star with Elvis Presley in his next film, 'Pot Luck.' Nancy will play a girl accountant who sorts out Elvis's tax problems. . . . Later in the year her own newly-formed film company, Boots Limited, hopes to begin production of 'The Flower Children.' Added Nancy: 'This is all about the LSD problem. I may appear in it with Sal Mineo.' " : : : Phil Ochs has changed to A&M records; Jim Kweskin & The Jug Band to Reprise.

Charlie Lloyd is recording an album live at the Fillmore for Atlantic (Chuck Berry also plans live sessions there, and Kama Sutra will be making records at the Avalon this summer). Rock fans are becoming more and more interested in those jazz musicians whose attitude and structural approach bring them close to the same artistic goals that rock aspires to. These "head-brothers" include Lloyd, Hugh Masekela, Gabor Szabo, and John Handy and their respective groups. More and more, the word "rock" is used to describe impact and intent, style, not specific musical content. Igor Stravinsky and Robert Johnson could both be called pre-Freedian rock artists.

The new Spencer Davis Group is Spencer Davis, Pete York, Eddie Hardin (organ, vocals), and Phil Sawyer (lead guitar)—note that "Somebody Help Me" and the entire *I'm a Man* lp are earlier SDG material, taken off several of the group's British albums. Stevie Winwood's new group has a single out on UA, "Paper Sun"—a very fine record, though not at all in what one might have thought was Stevie's style. The group is called Traffic, and the other members are David Mason (guitar, sitar), Chris Wood (flute), and James Capaldi (drums). Traffic and SDG will both be involved in writing and performing the music for a United Artists flick called *Here We Go Round the Mulberry Bush*.

At Malibu, Long Island, this summer: Young Rascals;

Blues Project & the Who; Association & Buffalo Springfield (July 14); Byrds (July 21); Doors (July 28); Jefferson Airplane (August 11); Mothers (August 18); Fugs & Yardbirds (August 25); Temptations (September 1). The Rheingold Concerts in Central Park include Stevie Wonder (July 12); Miracles (July 26); Byrds (July 28); Youngbloods & Neil Diamond (August 2); Blues Project & John Lee Hooker (August 9); Junior Wells, Son House, Jesse Fuller & "Big Boy" Crudup (August 25). Country Joe & the Fish at Cafe Au Go Go, NYC, August 1–6; new Al Kooper group late in August. The Electric Circus is open; Salvation opens very soon.

There's still no real rock scene in New York, but things are happening very fast (Rock Scully: "When I was here a month ago, New York was three years behind the Haight. Now it's two years behind"). The Grateful Dead came to town, and played so many free concerts that the SF tradition of music in the parks seems firmly established here. The Group Image has been a particularly important influence on the scene. (The Image are an amorphous bunch who produce music, posters, confusion, and other useful items. As yet, their music is nothing very good, but their performance is very enjoyable—the audience makes as much noise as the group and it's all very tribal and very real.) Monday nights at the Cheetah are now devoted to the Community, following a marvelous Grateful Dead–Group Image concert there early in June. For the first time, the Cheetah had good people on stage and good people in the audience, and it made all the difference in the world.

The Detroit Wheels, formerly with Mitch Ryder, are now recording for Impact Records. : : : Pete Townshend, of the Who, plans to record Tiny Tim (a Steve Paul perennial) for a British label.

The mono record will soon be obsolete, thanks to a recent price change that brought monaural and stereo records to the same list price. This should increase the importance of the 45 (because it now costs considerably less than an album, and is therefore more worthwhile) and force an increase in the quality of recording techniques, since lps will all be in stereo and more attention will be paid to sound. The quality of the albums themselves will also have to improve. The consumer who pays four dollars or so for an lp is going to expect an album full of good music, not just one hit and a handful of mud. Singles will still be vital for the promotion of albums, but albums will sell on their own strength, and groups that are only as good as their latest hit will lose out. We can expect, therefore, a growing separation between the lp market and the singles market.

This strong separation, where 45 rpm buyers purchase few lps if any, existed ten years ago; now it may return, but with a different emphasis. Rock, which has grown out of pop music, is now something larger. More rock albums are now sold than all other types of music put together, and that's a very significant fact. It means, first of all, that rock fans far outnumber enthusiasts of any other "type" of music; that, speaking either·democratically or economically, rock is now the vital music of the nation. Or, looking at it another way, it means that categories have less and less meaning every day, and rock, being the most eclectic and nonspecific musical category, is able to absorb more different tastes and preferences than any other music.

And it's easy to see where it's all going. 45's are for people who like a catchy melody, who have two or three favorite songs and that's what they'll go out of their way to buy—their interest in music is limited enough so they'll take whatever is fed to them over a transistor radio as long as it's sort of constant and doesn't intrude or demand too much. Easy listening. And that includes the subteens as well as the housewives, the people driving along listening to something-or-other, all of those to whom what's on the radio is not music but companionship or diversion or just stuffing to fill the emptiness in their ears when TV's not around. I know that feeling—quite recently I got hung up alone and listened to one radio station—and the same twenty-five songs—for more than twenty hours. I felt trapped. I'd turn it off, but first just one more song . . .

And later I realized it's a way of life. Many people get on the treadmill and just never get up to turn it off. Patterns are addictive. Rock is the new music, the music that changes but doesn't just change, that stays the same but doesn't only stay the same. It's frustrating to turn on a radio nowadays, because there isn't much rock—few songs that take you off the treadmill, few songs like "Somebody to Love," which even on the radio sounds as though this performance is unique, one of endless different ones—this song is flesh, not plastic.

But we're starting to get rock radio: stations playing album cuts, avoiding repetition, keeping maybe 100–150 songs on their playlist for the week and adding extras whenever they feel like it, people playing the records (instead of human machines, dj's who have been programed by the "program director" as though they were some sort of computer). KMPX-FM in San Francisco is the supreme example; but a clearer idea of the split that's taking place can be had by a comparison of two AM stations in that city.

KFRC, the leading "rock" station, has found that it has two listeners over eighteen for every teen-ager. Their reaction is caution: "We would probably avoid appealing to teens at the loss of our older audience." The notion, very probably correct, that's running through radio circles is that the people in their twenties who were listening to rock in their teens will stay with it now, as long as it doesn't get too harsh, or "psychedelic." So many successful rock stations play it very cool, tightening the playlist and seeing that things rock, but mildly. This sort of station will probably become more and more Top-40 oriented—"play what's popular," go for the widest possible audience base. Background music.

KYA, another SF rock station, is taking a different tack. In an attempt to program for an audience, and not just for a chart, they've started playing sixteen to nineteen records an hour, including heavy concentration on album cuts by local groups. In one hour I heard both sides of Big Brother's single, two Grateful Dead tracks (including "Morning Dew"), a Country Joe track (they play all seven minutes of "Section 43" frequently), a cut from the first Airplane album, "A Day in the Life," etc. KYA's latest ratings are the highest they've been in a year.

Sooner or later, I believe, all pop-rock stations will go one way or the other: plastic or flesh. Many of them are learning that their audience likes to listen, likes to have interesting music offered in a friendly, creative way, likes to hear songs they never heard before. And others are learning that they have an audience who won't tolerate intrusion on their security, who are willing to absorb five or six new songs a week, and that's the absolute most.

And what it all means is that you and I and other *Crawdaddy!* readers and kindred souls will be buying more and more lps, and will maintain our position of importance in the economy of the record industry, while slowly the singles market slips back into a mush morass of foot-tapping and heart-throbbing. But albums will be aimed more and more toward us, and more and more radio stations will change format to try to reach us. It's written in the numbers on the wall (*Billboard*, July 1): #1, *Sergeant Pepper;* #5, *Surrealistic Pillow;* #12, *Bob Dylan's Greatest Hits;* #17, *The Doors;* #38, *Between the Buttons;* #85, *Happy Jack;* #86, *The Grateful Dead;* #125, *Younger Than Yesterday;* #130, *Country Joe;* #144, *Moby Grape* . . . and much much much much more. A few months ago, no one—'cept maybe us—expected the Doors or the Airplane to have quite that much success. Now, comes the revolution; and I think we're winning . . .

Al Kooper, organist extraordinaire, has left the Blues Project to form his own group. His replacement is John-John McDuffey of the now-defunct King Bees. : : : The

Smile on the Face of the Tiger: Bob Dylan is likely to re-sign with Columbia Records after all (presumably with Bob Johnston continuing as his producer), despite his announced switch to MGM. Dylan hopes to record very soon; he has a great deal of material prepared. : : : *Don't Look Back,* a documentary film made while Dylan was touring Britain in 1965, is well worth your attention—one of the finest movies I've seen in a good while. It's extremely straight: no games, no cleverness, no moralizing or heavyhandedness. Instead, a *Blow-Up*-like feeling for a man's life; brilliant portraits of Albert Grossman, Donovan, Alan Price, the archetypal *Time* reporter, and of course Dylan himself.

The Butterfield Blues Band's third album will be out in a few weeks, at long last; the new members of the group are Charles Buggsy Maugh, bass; Gene Dinwiddie, tenor sax; and Keith Johnson, trumpet. : : : Mike Bloomfield's new group, while we're at it, is called the Electric Flag but will probably be going through its twelfth name change by the time you read this. Group members include Buddy Miles on drums; Harvey Brooks, bass; Nick Gravenites, vocals; Barry Goldberg, organ; Mike on lead and two horn-players whose names I just don't know.

A major indication of the growing importance and prestige of rock is the extent to which the mass media covered *Sergeant Pepper's Lonely Hearts Club Band,* and the way they covered it: not as a phenomenom, but as a work of art to review. *Life, Time, Newsweek, The New Yorker, The New York Times* all studied the album, and if nothing else at least recognized that the Beatles are indeed artists rather than a mere pop fad. This may be more-than-obvious, but it's still a major step forward for the mass media, who have always been culture snobs. The only review that really hurt was Richard Goldstein's in the Sunday *Times,* because with the opportunity to do so much good and turn so many people onto rock he got hung up on his own integrity and attempted to judge what he admittedly did not understand. It's okay not to understand, but Wrong to act as an interpreter for a language you don't speak. We sent the *Times* a note: "Dear NYT—You will of course receive a lot of letters. Let me say very simply that Richard Goldstein's lack of appreciation for *Sergeant Pepper* and the Beatles '67 is due to his trying too hard. He didn't 'relax and let the evening go.' Instead he stared through a microscope, and—curiously—he found things out of proportion. *Sergeant Pepper* is a show, a delightful entertainment—if there's a message it's 'Dig yourself'; but the boys don't push too hard . . . even 'Within You Without You' has laughter at the end, as if to say, 'Take us only as seriously as you want to.' Paul McCartney runs up to R. Goldstein screaming 'Good Morning! Good Morning!'; Richard scratches his head carefully and thinks: 'What did he mean by that?' He meant, 'good morning.' "

Beatle news: the next single may be "All We Need Is Love," the recording session of which was broadcast to the world via international television June 25 (with special guest M. Jagger). King Productions, in America, is producing a full-length feature cartoon about the Beatles, called *Yellow Submarine.* The score will include several past hits and some tracks from *Sergeant Pepper,* plus three new songs that the Beatles are recording especially for the film. Release is set for spring, 1968. And it looks very much as though Michelangelo Antonioni will direct the Beatles' third film, *Shades of a Personality,* shooting for which is scheduled to begin in Malaga, Spain, in September. The story line involves the four faces of a man (himself as dreamer, as seen by the world, as a member of mankind, as seen by himself), each played by a different Beatle. Meanwhile, the Beatles are trying to complete filming of a TV spectacular, and a new album, by early fall. Mmmm, such a flurry of activity!

Alex Hassilev and Mort Garson, independent producers, are making plans for a record label that will feature electronic music exclusively; the time seems right for good electronic stuff to succeed on the charts. Electronic commercials are also in the offing . . . : : : Phil Spector is still playing the music game; he just re-signed Ike & Tina Turner to his

Philles Records. If you don't own "River Deep" by now, blush.

The Monterey Pop Festival, contrary to some expectations, has produced nothing but good vibes: no one knows exactly how they plan to give away their 500G, but now that it's all over and it was beautiful and there was absolutely no trouble, everyone seems a little less up tight about the whole thing. Certainly, the festivals will continue. ABC-TV has filmed a color special about Monterey; the groups that played seem pretty pleased about what was going down; the music was everything from bad to excellent, including in the latter category the Who, Big Brother, Ravi Shankar, the Electric Flag, Steve Miller, Jimi Hendrix, and Otis Redding. See you next year.

Don Kirshner (former head of Colgems Records) is a man who blew it. He created the Monkees out of whole cloth, and he didn't miss a bet. The group succeeded in every way that Kirshner planned, and his finger was in every pie. What's more, despite being based on manipulation more than quality, the Monkees' success did not fade after the initial impact. It grew, and the entire music business admired Kirshner's ingenuity and envied him his percentage of the cake. Then, suddenly, it was all gone—Kirshner was fired from Colgems Records, and, shortly thereafter, lost his job at Screen Gems, whose highly successful music division he had been solely responsible for for five years.

What destroyed him? In a word, power. Kirshner has sued Columbia Pix Screen Gems for breach of contract, and Screen Gems' reply is very illuminating. Among other things, it charges that:

A) The night before the scheduled premiere of the Monkees TV show, Kirshner threatened not to deliver the master recordings for use on the series unless the producers of the show gave up their share of the music publishing royalties from Monkees songs, which share then reverted to Kirshner's operation.

B) Kirshner tried to force RCA to distribute as the new Monkees single a recording which, like most of the earlier ones, featured instrumental and vocal work by people other than the Monkees. This after the Monkees had decided to go straight, and had threatened to walk out on not only the record company but the television series if any record were released without their approval. (RCA followed the instructions of Screen Gems, not Kirshner, and refused to release the record; but only after spending $25,000 printing the jacket of the 45.)

C) Kirshner secretly tape-recorded conversations between himself, various officers of ColPix and Screen Gems, and the general manager of RCA. Etc., etc. Power blinds people. Legally, Colgems *couldn't* fire Kirshner; legally, the Monkees had no control over what was released under their name. But in actual fact, contractual obligations are only sheets of paper until it is established in court that the misconduct is in fact one-sided. And regardless of what the Monkees *must* do, if they refuse it may prove difficult to force them (shotgun recording sessions?). So Kirshner is in court instead of in charge, and the Monkees are in the studios doing what they want.

The Who got out of bed the morning after Jagger and Richards were convicted, announced that they considered the Stones "scapegoats for the rest of us," and made plans to record a series of Jagger-Richards compositions, to keep the Stones in the public eye while in jail. *The same morning* they recorded "Last Time"/"Under My Thumb." That afternoon, the single was pressed, and dubs were airlifted to the pirate radio stations, who immediately played them. The following morning the record was in stores across the country. Nice.

Mike Clark has reportedly left the Byrds, to be replaced by the drummer who was formerly with the Daily Flash. No confirmation yet.

The Doors. Photo by Elektra Records.

5: THE NIGHT ON FIRE

Rock Is Rock: A Discussion of a Doors Song

April 1967

Very few people have the balls to talk about "rock and roll" anymore. *Revolver* made it difficult. *Between the Buttons, Smile,* and the Doors lp are making it impossible. "Pop music" is definable only by pointing at a current chart; the Doors are not "pop," they are simply "modern music." The term applies not because rock has achieved the high standards of mainstream music, but conversely because rock has *absorbed* mainstream music, has become the leader, the arbiter of quality, the music of today. The Doors, Brian Wilson, the Stones *are* modern music, and contemporary "jazz" and "classical" composers must try to measure up.

The Doors is an album of magnitude. Thanks to the calm surefootedness of the group, the producer, the record company, there are no flaws; the Doors have been delivered to the public full grown (by current standards) and still growing (standards change). Gestation may have been long and painful; no one cares. The birth of the group is in this album, and it's as good as anything in rock. The awesome fact about the Doors is that they will improve.

So much for the review. This record is too good to be "explained," note by note, song by song; that sort of thing could only be boring, since the review would be immediately compared to the far-more-than-merely-communicative level of the work of art itself. Knowing that my reader is able to stop after any word I write and listen to all of "Light My Fire" before reading the next word, I should feel pretty foolish offering him a textual description of the buildup of erotic pressure in the performance. Is there really any point in saying something like, "The instrumental in 'Light My Fire' builds at the end into a truly visual orgasm in sound" when the reader can at any time put the album onto even the crummiest phonograph and experience that orgasm himself? Descriptive criticism is almost a waste of time, where quality is involved. It might be more valid for a reviewer to make a comment like: "The 'come' sequence at the end of 'Light My Fire' is the most powerfully controlled release of accumulated instrumental kineticism known on record, making even 'I'm a Man' by the Yardbirds a mere firecracker," but where that may make good reading and even makes pretty good writing under ordinary circumstances, in the context of an album as great and implicational and able-to-change-history as this one, comments like that dissatisfy and bore the reviewer, because to him they're simply obvious . . . That which can be simply stated is by its nature already known, and therefore not very interesting. To write about the unknown is exciting, unpredictable; to write about what you already know, even if you've only consciously known it a few minutes and you're pretty damn proud of your insight, can in the end be unstintingly boring.

Anyway, I've been thinking about "Blowin' in the Wind." A lot of people misunderstood that song, and it really is Dylan's fault. He shoved in lines like "How many times will the cannonballs fly," etc., which must have been practically *intended* to throw people off the track of what was being said. The line, "The answers my friends are blowin' in the wind" is so perfect that I doubt that anyone could hear it and not feel what is really being said (in fact, it's impossible to hear any true statement and not feel it correctly, although you may then go ahead and interpret it all wrong). But I'm not suggesting that the verses to "Blowin'" should have backed up the theme of the chorus line. The cumulative boredom that builds to a head and causes the creation of a line like "The answers are blowin' in the wind" (or, as we shall see, "Learn to forget") could not possibly then sustain the creation of an entire three verses or so of equal genius. Besides, three verses of equal genius would destroy the impact. No, I only say that the public-at-large should not have been maligned by a deliberate attempt to throw them off the track, an attempt made only because Dylan 1962 realized that he could, with delightful ease, present great truth to the world at large and make it invisible to them at the same time. Like most crimes, it was perpetrated because the criminal knew he could get away with it.

But ignoring for now the clumsy camouflage of the verses, it really is difficult to carefully misinterpret "Blowin' in the Wind" . . . its meaningfulness even overshadows its own ambiguity! If we assume that "The answers are blowin' in the wind" means that the answers are inaccessible, hard to hold onto, out of reach, then the words are saying that we have no answers to work with; they're unobtainable, and therefore we must reject our need for answers and work without them. If, on the other hand, the listener reacts to the concept of "blowin' in the wind" as implying accessibility, the total *availability* of all answers, we interpret the phrase as implying the uselessness of mere answers and availability—toss all top-secret data out the window; we have all the answers, and still haven't got any truth. These answers, therefore, accessible as they are, are mere truths-in-context, i.e., they are true whenever they are placed within a context in which they are true. They don't achieve anything. We can't work with them because they are too all-present and part-of-what-clearly-is, and therefore we must work without them. These two opposite interpretations of "blowin' in the wind" as a phrase inevitably lead to the same conclusion because the two are both part of the statement "The answers my friends are blowin' in the wind," which has only one meaning.

Proof: the subject matter of such a statement must be the availability of knowledge. So Dylan is either saying (i.e., the words are saying) "I know everything," or "I know nothing," or he wouldn't bring up the subject. Since it is highly improbable that one would know everything, and more improbable that one would bother writing a song about it if one did, and anyway unlikely that we would have any trouble recognizing such a song were it written, we can be very certain that the song says: "I (we) know nothing." Which is the feeling one gets from the line "The answer . . . wind" before one even starts going through all this reasoning. The vibrations from the line are very strong; you're probably thinking that I'm fooling around right now, that if I felt like it I could prove anything; that fact, however, does not imply that I *would* prove anything, since if I tried to prove a falsehood the vibrations—what you "know" to be true about something, in other words—would make my words no matter how clever feel like lies. How much we rely on our instincts! If you think a song is good I could never convince you it's bad, and that means in effect that though anything can be proven, little if anything can be affected by proofs. And no matter how you react to a thought like "blowin' in the wind" (accessibility or inaccessibility) you do not change your assumptions about the full phrase—you merely change your thought process to fit the way you feel. When asked what the words "blowin' in the wind" meant, Dylan was unable to answer, was in fact amazed at being asked. "They mean: blowin' in the wind." In concert in Boston he got the lines to the verses mixed up, but he didn't seem to think *that* was very important.

"Soul Kitchen" is nice. It is so reminiscent of "Blowin' in the Wind" in terms of message that one almost expects Peter Paul & Mary to make it a Top 40 smash. It's just a nice little song about desire, a routine drama in which Jim points out that it looks like it's time for him to go (beautiful posturing: twiddling of thumbs, glance at the clock, well, um, looks like it's time for me to leave, uh . . .) but he'd "really like to stay here all night." And he does stay, and the Doors do their usual "boy gets girl" instrumental routine, and then Jim lampoons his own posturing, repeating, "The clock says it's time to close now," but then saying, "I *know* I've got to go now." "I'd really like to stay here *all night*" changes from effective plea into bitter irony; the words that meant "let me in" before mean "sorry, baby" after. And that's almost all there is to it, except that the plea "Let me sleep all night in your soul kitchen" is so fantastically strong. Jim obviously didn't give that much of a damn about the girl in this case, so something else must have been bothering him. The intensity of that plea could not have been faked. And this leads us to the really stunning revelation that sexual desire is merely a particular instance of some more far-reaching grand dissatisfaction.

The message of "Soul Kitchen" is of course "Learn to forget," a "message"/phrase at least as powerful as "The answers my friends are blowin' in the wind" and very similar in the sort of implications and emotions it conjures up. The actual words "learn to forget" are repeated four times at the end of the second verse of "Soul Kitchen," and are never returned to in any way. In fact, the band seems to be unaware of them, and Robbie has been known to say that he considers the piece inconsequential! And as compared with the Dylan song, a great deal of the success of this one is due to the fact that the playing, and the words of the song other than "learn to forget," are almost totally unrelated to the message, and as a result they serve as emphasis rather than confusion. So this truth is totally accessible to anyone listening to the song—and the irony here is that the song is not a single, not a huge airplay hit, not being heard by more than maybe 20,000 people. [Well, the album turned out to be a #1 smash, so revise that upwards by a couple of decimal points . . .]

"Learn to forget"—what power that phrase has! It's possible to get stoned for days listening to this song . . . for a while it will seem the one truth available to us. It eventually recedes, of course, into merely a tantalizing command:

within the song it's a posthypnotic suggestion to the girl being seduced, it's a bitter comment on the necessity of learning to forget in order to get along in this grubby world, it's a statement of faith in the ability of man to will what he doesn't want out of existence. Above all, it's an echo of the Sophoclean section of "The End" (echo because the album is programed circularly for repeated listenings), in which it becomes necessary to kill the father. As Paul Rothchild says in *Crawdaddy!* 10, " 'Kill the father' means kill all of those things within yourself that are instilled in you and are not of yourself." Obviously, "learn to forget," which comes from the mouth of the same man, could easily have the same meaning to Jim. But "The End," which is a truly beautiful, perfected, polished intellectual statement, cannot communicate as powerfully as "Soul Kitchen," since the latter is not on an intellectual level at all. "The End" is great to listen to when you're high (or any other time), but "Soul Kitchen" will get you high, which is obviously much cruder and more important. "Soul Kitchen," with its revelation that sexual desire is more complexly motivated than we think (all right, suppose it's immediately caused by the animal instinct for survival through reproduction of the self; the implications of *that* are that sexual desire is within each person that individual's expression of the agony of being and the relationship between man and the future, that is to say, the meaning of life. If I want that girl because deep down I want to assure my own survival through descendants, then that look in my eyes reflects all the pain of the question: why do I want descendants, why does man consider time a rival he must conquer? That makes sexual need [as opposed to lust] the purest form of spiritual pain known to man, and therefore the most beautiful thing around), and its fantastically ambiguous "learn to forget" . . . "Soul Kitchen," because it conjures up this kind of stuff, is a catalyst with more potential for generating truth—in my opinion—than anything since middle Faulkner.

It's important now to realize that the "the answers my friends are blowin' in the wind" phrase itself has as much potential for truth generation, within the right context, as "learn to forget." The greater value of "Soul Kitchen," which happens to contain the latter, has something to do with the triumph of rock. Rock, which is less cognitive, allows the creator of the vehicle for the phrase more freedom in subject. "Folk" basically demands a relationship between all words and ideas in a song, unless nonsense words are used, whereas rock may be as totally noncognitive without being nonsense as "Hey ninety-eight point six the love that was the medicine that saved me, oh I love my baby." Rock gave Jim Morrison the freedom to slip "learn to forget" into the middle of a seduction song, which offers no distraction at all, whereas Dylan in order to even *say* that the answers are blowing in the wind had to provide some representative questions. "Soul Kitchen" has the further advantage, common in rock, that you can't hear all the words, so you can pretty much contextualize as you like. And the direct appeal to the mind made by "folk" (straightforward words, guitar, voice) cannot compare, it seems to me, with the abilities of rock to move people's muscles, bodies, caught up and swaying and moving so that a phrase like "learn to forget" can actually become your whole body, can sink into your soul on a more-than-cognitive level. Rock, because of the number of senses it can get to (on a dance floor, eyes, ears, nose, mouth, and tactile) and the extent to which it can pervade those senses, is really the most advanced art form we have.

Rothchild Speaks

March 1967

This interview was taped in Englewood, New Jersey, in March 1967, shortly after the release of the first Doors album, which

Paul Rothchild produced. Last names are used throughout to avoid ambiguity.

WILLIAMS: How the hell does Krieger play so slow? ROTHCHILD: Well, it's understandable when you consider that most blues players in the new music—the new rock—today base their guitar techniques on a blues foundation, either a Chicago blues or a delta blues tradition, or on almost a folk cotton-picking technique. Robbie doesn't. His technique, his original guitar-playing technique, comes from flamenco music, which was his first guitar music. And a firm knowledge of the use of—in classical music—rubato is essential in flamenco music, being able to sustain on one note and then move over very smoothly and easily to another note without a lot of flamboyance. This is true in slow flamenco music. Most people are familiar with rapid flamenco techniques, a lot of fireworks and brilliance, but on the slow tunes you've got to be able to handle slow tones very quickly and almost make it seem that one note is continuing while you're actually playing to another note.

Also, if you watch Robbie play, even when he's playing very quickly he looks like he's playing slowly—if you watch his face he looks up casually—he always looks as if some-body's just asked him a question and he's thinking very seriously about what the answer might be.

WILLIAMS: I get the feeling that most lead guitarists either want to hear themselves playing the melody or hear them-selves doing a rhythm thing, and it's inconceivable to me that Robbie could even be listening to himself—I mean he knows exactly what he's doing, but he's playing something which is so whole with the music. ROTHCHILD: The point is that Robbie isn't listening to himself when he plays, he's listening to Ray. More than anything he's listening to Ray. But since there are only two voicing instruments in the group, and since Ray is responsible more than any other instrument for the rhythm—the melodic rhythm rather than the drums, which have the solid rhythm—Robbie's got to fill in all of the musical question marks which are left open. So he is listening a great deal and not tremendously interested in the whole lot of ego play that guitar players get into.

WILLIAMS: The integration is unbelievable, because he never does a virtuosity thing, all the way through "The End" you're never once conscious of the guitar, which is practically the only instrument that's playing—you know, except for the drums, which are doing a very different thing —because he never . . . the only virtuosity stuff at all is in "Light My Fire," where it's for a reason, it's a virtuosity song.

Tell me what you know about the history of the group. ROTHCHILD: I actually know very little. I know that Ray Manzarek and Jim Morrison started performing together when they were both students at the film school at UCLA. They were friends from the film department and they found out they both had an interest in music and they started to perform. Their early music was mostly blues with Ray doing a tremendous amount of the singing, interestingly enough. WILLIAMS: Did Jim play anything at that time? ROTHCHILD: No. And I don't even know where Robbie came from or how he fitted into the group. I've never really been tremendously interested myself in the past social-musical activities of groups. The questions I usually ask musicians are about their musical past, their training, what their influences are, where they get their reasons, their musical reasons. As for where they came from, and how they got together . . . they did all get together at the University of California at Los Angeles, and, well, they were playing together as long ago as about two and a half years, I guess. As the Doors they've been playing together for a little over a year now, a year and a half . . . And it's, uh, a constantly changing and moving process for them.

It's a relief for them to have this first album out because

it gives them an opportunity to move on towards music and musical concepts that they've been discussing and wanting to get into. This is a very interesting thing that a lot of groups have, the effect that making albums has on them, and how it's almost an insistence that they change their repertoire. It's like a group goes into a recording studio and that giant performance mirror, the tape recorder, is put in front of them, they finally work out all of the problems and all of the fine points in the music that they've been wanting to for so long, and then when they get through with the tunes a great many of them fall by the wayside. The statement's been made.

WILLIAMS: The material's never as good as on the first album for a lot of groups. ROTHCHILD: That's right. And it's almost a kind of catharsis for the musicians to make their first album because it frees them, in many respects; it allows them to go to the other places they've been wanting to for so long but they've been tied down to their original material. This may sound strange to use words like "tied down" but it's really true; now the Doors, since they are a creative and performing group, are forced—and they enjoy it—to look forward to their next album. That means we have to get on to the new material. That doesn't mean they stop performing the old stuff, the best of it remains in the repertoire . . .

WILLIAMS: Which are the earliest songs on the album? ROTHCHILD: "I Looked at You" and "Take It as It Comes." Those represent probably the genesis of the group, more than any others. The newer of the tunes are the ones that are deeper, the ones that show a greater maturity. "The End" is newer. "The End," it's interesting, "The End" was always a changing piece. Jim used it as a, almost an open canvas for his poetic bits and pieces and fragments and images and little couplets and things that he just wanted to say, and it changed all the time, it was always a changing thing. Now it rarely changes. Now that it's on record and the musicians can listen to it on record it is the statement they wanted to make and Jim tends to perform it that way. Sometimes he'll leave something out, sometimes he will put something else in but now it's a formed piece, it isn't that open canvas any more. And because of this, Jim commented to me recently, the thing he's most deeply concerned with right now is opening another canvas of that nature, something as broad in concept as "The End."

WILLIAMS: On interpreting "The End": I considered for the first time the other day that the lines "This is the end my only friend" and particularly "It hurts to set you free but you'll never bother me"—it occurred to me, when I heard that, that the song might be about a murder, and not just a guy leaving a girl. The possibility opened that the whole thing was the murderer's mind and ah, the stream of consciousness starting from and leading back *to* . . . ROTHCHILD: It's interesting that you say that, because Jim is fascinated with the concept of death. He's interested in spiritual deaths, conceptual deaths, more than physical deaths actually, you'll find this theme in many of his songs, uh, the line "The end of nights we tried to die" . . . WILLIAMS: That goes right back to "Crystal Ship." ROTHCHILD: Exactly.

Uh, I'm not sure if this is what Jim has in mind but it's almost as if Jim is saying . . . realize this is my interpretation and not Jim's, 'cause I've never asked Jim, he presented it to me and said it's for your head, interpret it as you will, Jim's saying almost as a friend, okay, my friend and I take an acid trip, and then I say to my friend this is the end my friend, my only friend, the end of laughter and soft lies, the end of nights we tried to die, ah, the line, the end of nights we tried to die, to my mind is a direct reference to the concept that most psychedelics are a form of physical poisoning, that chemicals are a means of reorienting the body through a kind of poison . . .

WILLIAMS: You're saying this is the end, during the trip or before it? ROTHCHILD: The way I feel it, the trip has started and he's saying this is the end. WILLIAMS: As a beginning. ROTHCHILD: Right. This is the end. He has had a realization concerning a relationship, now this can be far more universal than a statement to this theoretical friend who is right there, this could be the end of the world, the end of laughter and soft lies, or the end of— WILLIAMS: Himself.

ROTHCHILD: Precisely. He's saying okay here's a trip, every time we take a trip there's a death—of concepts, of bullshit, a death of laughter and soft lies, let's get real with ourselves, let's get real with each other, um . . . there's one thing Jim used to say during the song which is just a stark death image. It was the blue bus theory, but it was stated in a different way, and he used to use them both, he used the blue bus thing and he'd also say, uh, "Have you seen the accident outside, seven people took a ride and something something something and seven people died," which is really very groovy, "have you seen the accident outside"—the world—seven people took a ride, this trip, looked at the world, and died. All of that that they saw in themselves which before lived, in other words the bullshit concept of the world which had been burned into their brains since childhood, had to die. And with every end there is a beginning, it is a cyclical thing, the end always has in it inherent a beginning, uh, trying to remember . . . "Can you picture what will be so limitless and free, desperately in need of some stranger's hand in a desperate land." Things are very wrong out there so let us kill ourselves or those things in ourselves that are false, that are bullshit, the false giddiness, the TV giddiness, canned audience reaction laughter—there's more humor in the world than needs to be created scientifically in a TV studio, I'm babbling I understand but I'm on as much of a hunch trying to explain as Jim is who's trying to lay it down.

Of the other imagery in the song, the little poetic bits between the double verse section in the beginning and the double verse section in the end, you have things like the snake—well there he's saying just get down to reality, the snake thing of course is just pure sexual imagery (to my mind), ride the snake to the ancient lake, that comes right out of Negro imagery, blues imagery, which Jim is very familiar with, "the snake he's old and his skin is cold," what he is saying is okay let's get down to the realities of life, there are very few realities and one of the few truly real realities is sexual awareness and companionship, Jim is very lucid in that department. . . . Oh right, and the first one which is very beautiful, "lost in a Roman"—oh, a piece of beautiful classical imagery—"lost in a Roman wilderness of pain." To my mind all I can see is great crumbling ruins of a great civilization, which of course flashes right back to now, "lost in a Roman wilderness of pain and all the children are insane," repeated. WILLIAMS: The barbarians. ROTHCHILD: Right. "Waiting for the summer rain," let's get cleansed, let's get cleansed, people. Another symbolic death by the way. Insanity of course is a symbolic death, it's a death itself, and the cleansing is a rebirth. And then of course there's the incredible Oedipal thing in the middle which is the first giant build, and I have talked with Jim about that, because I have rarely been as impressed . . .

I have never been as moved in a recording studio as I was when that take went down. I was impressed by the fact that for one of the very first times in rock-and-roll history sheer drama had taken place on tape. This to me is very important, and it's also significant that Jim has used, chose to use a purely classical image (in modern dress) to do this. The story he tells is basically the Oedipus legend, ah, the killer awoke before dawn, he put his boots on, he chose a face from the ancient gallery and he walked on down the hall. And he came to a door and he walked inside, and he went to the room where his brother lived, and then he went into the room where his sister lived, and then walked on down the hall, and he came to a door and he walked inside and he said, father, yes son, I want to kill you, and then he walked— WILLIAMS: No, no, it just immediately becomes mother . . . ROTHCHILD: Yes, there's a little musical thing, and then he says mother I want to and then he screams. He screams for obvious reasons, there are even for Jim cultural limitations.

WILLIAMS: And it's more effective. ROTHCHILD: Of course, it's more effective, it's basic, it's primal, it's the reason, it's the motivation. Jim is saying, and Jim has phrased it precisely this way, kill the father, fuck the mother, and at one point Jim said to me during the recording session, he was very emotionally moved, and he was wondering, and he was tearful, and he shouted in the studio, "Does *anybody* understand me?" And I said yes I do, and right then and there we got into a long discussion about just what does this mean, this section, and Jim just kept saying over and over, kill the father, fuck the mother, and essentially it boils down to just this, kill the father means kill all of those things in yourself which are instilled in you and are not of yourself, they are not your own, they are alien concepts which are not yours, they must die, those are the things that must die. The psychedelic revolution. Fuck the mother is very basic, and it means get back to the essence, what is the reality, what is, fuck the mother is very basically mother, mother-birth, real, very real, you can touch it, you can grab it, you can feel it, it's nature, it's real, it can't lie to you.

So what he says at the end of the Oedipus section, which is essentially the same thing that the classic says, he is saying, kill the alien concepts, get back to reality, which is precisely what the song is about, the end, the end of alien concepts, the beginning of personal concepts. Get to reality, get to your *own* reality, get to your *own* in-touch-with-yourself situation . . .

WILLIAMS: I was just thinking in terms of getting back to reality, taking that against "Soul Kitchen," with the plea, desperation, the message, it's a message song, "Soul Kitchen" has got to be a message song, learn to forget, in a way, in its totality maybe it implies the opposite. ROTHCHILD: Well,

"Soul Kitchen" of course is full of sexual imagery. WILLIAMS: But it even goes beyond, you learn to forget, goes beyond everything else in that song and that's the reverse. ROTHCHILD: "Learn to forget" is of course the key in there, otherwise Jim would not be saying it so many times in the song, ah, this is something, this is another aspect of the revolution, it goes back to the same thing as "The End"—learn to forget the bullshit, the alien concepts, get back to reality, sleep in the soul kitchen. WILLIAMS: Although to me it's not as direct as "Soul Kitchen," it says something else too, it's very painful, everything he says in "Soul Kitchen" is very painful for him to say the way he says it, and learn to forget is very bitter. ROTHCHILD: Well, let's look at it this way: "Soul Kitchen" is an earlier song. And Jim hadn't learned to forget nearly as well as he did later on when he did "The End."

. . . ROTHCHILD: I wonder if I'm even talking loud enough for that thing. WILLIAMS: We'll check it . . . Say that again for the Sony people. ROTHCHILD: We're using this little Sony tape recorder here to record me saying all this blither, and it just occurred to me that the recordings I'm making these days are recorded with Sony microphones. All the producers in the country will dig that. WILLIAMS: We'll send a copy to Sony . . . ROTHCHILD: That's where the groovy drum sound comes from. WILLIAMS: How so, how does the mike affect the pickup of the sound? ROTHCHILD: Well, everybody is familiar with how different loudspeakers affect the sound of a recording, each has a different characteristic, this is even more apparent with microphones.

Once you get to know microphones, each mike has a different characteristic and can do a specific job better than another mike. There are certain microphones which are great for recording voice, there are others which are excellent for recording strings, or trumpets, or drums or electric guitars, and it's a nice thing to know which microphone to use for what function. If you've got a very loud brass section, one of the best microphones to use is one of the oldest mikes in

existence, an old RCA 44, the old radio announcer's microphone that everybody is familiar with, a great huge lump of
metal, the old octagonal mike. It's probably the smoothest
mike in the world, with no high end of it, that's why brass
sounds so good.

WILLIAMS: Do you bring your own mikes into a studio?
ROTHCHILD: No, we use studios with microphone comple-
ments that are consistent with our recording techniques. Most
good recording studios have certain kinds of microphones,
they have Sonys, or Neumans, or Telefunkens or Capps or
Synchrons, and the RCA mikes, plus the world's cheapest
microphone, which is probably used on every bass drum in
the world. That's the Altex 633-C, which I think costs $30,
which is the greatest bass drum mike in the world, everybody
uses it, it's called a salt-shaker mike.

WILLIAMS: What are the aspects of picking a recording
studio for a specific group other than the microphones: the
size? the sound echo feeling? . . . what is it? ROTHCHILD: The
engineers are the most important factor in any studio. Just
as an artist will look for a creative producer, a producer will
look for a creative engineer. That's vital. You can have the
greatest recording studio in the world and, I have been in
them with an inferior engineer, you might just as well have
done it on this Sony and come up with a far greater sound.

Once you know you've got a good engineer to work with,
you must be sure that the tools that he has available are
excellent. I recently worked with one of the world's great
engineers who was, until recently, strapped by one of the
worst studios in the country as far as I'm concerned for the
kind of recording I like to do. Dave Hassinger is a perfect example of a great engineer in a bad studio. He became very
famous for his work with the Stones. Hassinger is truly one
of the great engineers in the world today, but I feel he was
strapped by one of the worst recording studios in the country,
the now-famous RCA Victor Studio B in Hollywood, a

colossus of an antique. It's so far behind the times it's really sad; that Hassinger was able to go as far as he did with that studio is a mark of his excellence as an engineer. A better proof of Hassinger's excellence as an engineer, just as a pure creative engineer, regardless of what people think of the record, the music, is the work he did with the Electric Prunes, which he did from the ground up. Now that's Hassinger, all Hassinger. He did *not* record that at RCA Studio B, which is why it sounds so modern. That was recorded at Goldstar and parts of it were recorded at Sunset. Listen to the A side of the new Love record, *Da Capo,* which was recorded by Hassinger in Studio B, a miracle of engineering, a miracle of engineering . . .

WILLIAMS: The sessions on this album, how did they start, when did they start? ROTHCHILD: Whew, you would have to ask me questions about time and space. August and September, I think. We recorded for two weeks and mixed for five. WILLIAMS: I'm interested more in details of the session, that is, how it went, walking into the studios for the first time . . .

ROTHCHILD: I'll tell you exactly. They had done a demo for Columbia and then I went to work with them for Elektra, preparing them. This is something I like to do with what I consider to be new groups, virgin groups, who have not been in studios before, because there are all kinds of problems that have to be resolved with groups before they can get down to the business of making phonograph records comfortably. The common concept for recording studios—which is not mine—is that recording studios are hospitals where musicians go to have their music operated on. I like to get away from that as completely as possible and try to convert the atmosphere and the emotion of the studio into one which is more warm, let's sit around the living room and play music for a while, not even let's sit around the club and play music for a while which is also a little alien. Music is and always will be a very personal experience. WILLIAMS: Well, that changes from group to group . . . ROTHCHILD: Oh yes, of course, don't misunderstand me, a rock and roll group needs to have an audience to react against; in a recording studio that audience becomes a very specific audience, it's the producer.

He's got to fulfill many functions as an audience. Rather than sitting there and clapping his hands or booing, there are other ways he shows his delight or criticism. What we did, in order to break the cherry of this group in the recording studio, as it were, what I generally like to do is go into the studio first with the musicians feeling that they're going in for a session. *I* realize that we're going to blow a day or two, but we go in to cut masters, we don't go in to screw around. Sometimes you get lucky. We went in and we cut two tunes, neither of which appear on this record. We don't stop at a perfect take, we stop at a take that has the muse in it. That's the most important thing: the take must have the feel, must have the musical feel in it, even if there are musical errors. When the muse comes into the studio to visit us, that's the take . . .

WILLIAMS: How was it, recording "The End"? ROTHCHILD: It was beautiful, it was one of the most beautiful moments I've ever had in a recording studio, that half hour when "The End" was recorded. I was emotionally wrung. Usually as a producer you sit there listening for all the things that are right and all of the things that are about to go wrong. You're following every instrument simultaneously, you're following the feeling, the mood, all the way through. In this take I was completely, I was absolutely audience. I had done my job, there was nothing actually for me to do once the machines were rolling. I had made sure the sound was right on each instrument, you know, when we did our setup; Bruce, the engineer, had been cued by me on everything that I wanted him to do, and at the beginning of the take I was sitting there—producer—listening to take.

Midway through I was no longer producer; I was just completely sucked up into it. When we recorded it the studio was totally darkened, the only lights visible were a candle burning in the recording studio right next to Jim, whose back was to the control room, singing into his microphone, and the lights on the v.u. meters in the control room. All the other lights were off . . . it was . . very dark . . . . ha . .

WILLIAMS: What studio? ROTHCHILD: Sunset Sound Recorders, what I feel to be the best studio in the country right now, mainly because of Bruce Botnick who's twenty-three years old and one of the grooviest engineers I can conceive of, extraordinarily creative and very pleasant to work with. Ah, and Jim . . . it was a magic moment . . . Jim was doing "The End," he was just doing it, for all time, and I was pulled off, right on down his road, he said come with me and I did. It was almost a shock when the song was over, you know when Robbie plays those last little tinkling notes on the guitar. It felt like, yeah, you know, like, yes, it's the end, *that*'s the end, it cannot go any further, that's the statement.

I felt emotionally washed. There were four other people in the control room at that time, when the take was over and we realized the tape was still going. Bruce, the engineer, was completely sucked along into it and instead of sitting there at attention the way engineers are wont to do, his head was on the console and he was just—immersed. Just absolutely immersed in this take. And he'd done it all, and he'd made all the moves right, because Bruce and I had established a kind of rapport, he knew where I wanted things done and when, and when his work was done he did exactly the same thing, involuntarily, without volition, he didn't know he was going to do it but he became audience too. So the muse *did* visit the studio that time. And all of us were audience, there was nothing left, the machines knew what to do I guess. It was all right.

WILLIAMS: Jim recorded it on acid? ROTHCHILD: No, not that one. The night before . . . we tried the night before, we attempted the night before to record "The End," and we couldn't get it. Jim couldn't do it. He wanted desperately to do it, his entire being was screaming "Kill the father, Fuck the mother! Kill the father, Fuck the mother!" Now I don't know, have you heard him saying in the middle of "The End" during that big "come" part, have you heard him saying, "kill, kill, kill"? WILLIAMS: I hear words, I can't tell what they are. ROTHCHILD: You'll hear it next time. During the whole giant raga thing he's going "kill! kill! kill! kill!" and at another point he's going "Fuck, fuck," as a rhythm instrument, the rhythm's going (bangs on microphone) fuck, fuck, fuck, that's down on the track too, as a rhythm instrument, which is what we intended it to be.

Now, I'm sure that clinically Jim was still on an acid trip; but it was done on the after period, the lucid . . . I guess it isn't the lucid, the clear light period, it's the reflective period of an acid trip. But I have tried several times to record artists on acid and it doesn't work. At least, it doesn't work for me. I have never seen it work in a studio; I have never spoken with a producer who has tried it and has been successful.

WILLIAMS: Maybe the most interesting question is how did "The End" come to be; how much of it had been like that before; and how much of it just suddenly bloomed in those two nights? ROTHCHILD: Let's put it this way: the frame, the structure of the song was set in everyone's mind, everyone knew what had to be done. Ray knew what he was going to play, not the notes, but where and why it had to be, Robbie knew where and why, John—a brilliant drummer, "The End" proved that, in my book that's some of the greatest drumming I've ever heard in my life, irrespective of the fact that I'm involved in this album it's incredibly creative drumming—has an instinct for when. During a very quiet part he'll just come in with three drum shots that are about as loud as you can hit a drum, and they're right, they're absolutely right! Now, you can't plan those things.

Jim, of course, in the recesses of his creative self knew exactly what the song had to be. It went through several permutations in the studio. He'd reach into his back pocket and pull out a sheaf of miscellaneous scraps of paper that had little notes on them, little lines of poetry, and he'd look at them, crumple them up and throw them away, and sing different lines during the tune, lines I'd heard him sing in a club. Other times he'd just riff something I'd never heard before, some of which appears on the record. The version you hear on the record is I think a finalized form, it's almost exactly the way they perform it on stage now. It's one of those rare things where a piece of music was caught at the peak of its maturity in a recording studio, extremely rare. The usual situation is that it was recorded too soon or too late, more frequently it was recorded too late. There's a kind of lethargy you hear in a lot of recorded performances that is the result of a piece of music not being caught at its prime, but in its old age. When everybody has their things down pat and there isn't the enthusiasm of creativity.

. . . ROTHCHILD: "Alabama Song," I'm sure you want to know about that. Both Ray and Jim are admirers of Kurt Weill and Bertold Brecht. For obvious reasons. I guess Brecht was saying in the thirties what Morrison is trying to say in the sixties. They're completely different messages, but both trying to declare a reality to their generation. It's sort of the Doors' tribute to another time, another brave time for some other brave men. And the lyric to "Alabama Song" is strangely contemporary. There is one other verse in the "Alabama Song" which the Doors don't sing, the verse missing is "Show us the way to the next little dollar, oh, don't ask why." And *that* is out of context for the Doors, that's not quite what they had in mind . . .

And, in addition, there is a strange instrument on that

tune. It comes from about the nineteen-twenties; it's a variant of the autoharp. Instead of being strummed or plucked it's struck. The instrument is called a Marxaphone, it was patented under that name. It's a series of steel springs that are located at an angle above the strings; you push down on the steel springs and a little metal hammer at the end goes buoong— It's a percussion instrument, a percussion autoharp. Ray played it on an overdub. . . . Overdubbing literally means to take your original track and add onto it, putting sound on top of it. Today the system is called sel-synch, it stands for selective synchronization. You can record onto an open track, in synch with the other music.

WILLIAMS: In reference to which, Jim grunts throughout, particularly on "Back Door Man"—his grunts at the beginning are great, just great. And constant noise, throughout "The End" and a lot in "Light My Fire." Does he just have an open mike he can do anything into, you just mix it down because it's on a separate track? ROTHCHILD: That's right. The lead vocalist is always on a track by himself so that you have absolute flexibility, because listening in a recording studio the perspective's always wrong for making a balanced mix. You're generally listening at very high levels on superb speakers, and unless you can supply everybody in the United States with Altex 605 speakers you're in a world of trouble. So you've got to have absolute flexibility, especially over your lead singer and if you're lucky as n.any other elements as you can in your recording . . . Jim, especially if you see him live, likes to grab the microphone and, uh, he kinda works himself up to a song. He'll grab the microphone and he'll go "unh," "gaa," "yeaa," and he goes through almost a whole pagan ritual. It's a modern West Coast psychedelic invocation of the muse.

. . . On "End of the Night," Jim decided at the last minute to change the lyric on that. It was originally, and always had been, "take a trip into the end of the night" and at that point Jim decided that the word "trip" had been violently overused, so he changed it to "highway." "End of the Night" is another paean to the, well, it's Jim saying to the world come on, people, get free, get rid of all that shit, take a journey to the great midnight. I'm sure that has meaning for me, and I'm sure that has meaning for you, and I'm sure our meanings are a great deal different. Jim likes to do that.

Brian Wilson. Photo by Linda Eastman.

6: BRIAN

A Celebration of *Wild Honey*

January 1968

When David Anderle and I began our discussion of Brian Wilson, we had just finished listening to *Wild Honey* (The Beach Boys, Capitol Records, November 1967) for about the second time. We were depressed. We both count ourselves among the World's Most Loyal Brian Wilson Fans—David worked with Brian and the Beach Boys in 1966–1967, as a friend, as an advisor in the realm of business, as the head of Brother Records (the Beach Boys' own record company)—but we just couldn't see *anything* in this new album. This is reflected in our comments throughout the interview.

I haven't talked with David, but I'm sure he's changed his mind. *Wild Honey* is one of last year's finest albums, a lovely record full of exuberant singing and beautiful, evocative music. The best that can be said for the lyrics is that they don't get in the way (though they are masterfully inappropriate at times). The instrumentation and overall sound are crude as can be—the record was no doubt recorded in Brian's home studio. But very few things can stand in the way of really fine music, and this record is the triumph of the creative musician over the incredible hassles of the music world.

Hooray!

— — — — — — — — — — — — —

I'm just sitting and thinking, pulling things together. I wouldn't dream, at this point, of trying to do a significant article on Paul Williams; I know nothing about him. And yet I've somewhere got the idea that I can write about the Beach Boys. Fun, Fun, Fun. God Only Knows. The Beach

117

Boys relate to my very core, little else; can I write about that?

I came across the Beach Boys when I was most alone. Not lonely, I don't mean that; but no one listened to my albums. Music was part of my most private world: Harvard Square after 1 A.M., walking the sides of highways, New York a day at a time, *Blonde on Blonde* late into the afternoon and later. No one talked to me about music; people talked to me about the magazine and the weather, when they talked at all. But Derek Taylor wrote an article in *Hit Parader,* and Al Kooper at Newport mentioned *Pet Sounds* as his favorite record, and "God Only Knows" sounded good on eight transistors, and eventually I bought the album. Eagerly and reluctantly. After all, the Beach Boys?

The Beach Boys. In a week, *Pet Sounds* was my closest friend. Even today only *Pet Sounds,* "If Only We Knew" (John Handy), and "Sad-Eyed Lady" can really calm my nerves. Walking sandy shores. I don't know what I find in this music, but it's always there: warmness, serenity, friendship. Strength. I decided *Pet Sounds* was the best rock album yet with no advice from anyone and I never changed my mind. At some point a person sets up his own aesthetic standards, which can't be justified, can't be questioned; I began this process for myself with *Pet Sounds.* It doesn't have reasons, it's a starting point. Foundation stone. A few decisions shape our lives.

————————————

Celebration. *Smile* is the album that never was, and *Smile* is the reason that David and I were slow to respond to *Wild Honey.* We expected more. We expected more, in fact, than we would expect from any other composer alive, because the tracks we'd heard from *Smile* were just that good. *Smiley Smile* was the record put out instead of *Smile,* when that fell through; a confusion, a record with a few of *Smile's* songs, changed around quite a bit, but almost none of the tracks prepared for the earlier album. And *Wild Honey* is just another Beach Boys record, which is only to say that it's not *Smile,* and it was necessary for us to forget *Smile* before we could appreciate what came later.

Well, no. *Smile* is not forgotten, never will be. But I am comfortable with *Wild Honey* now, love *Wild Honey* now, because it is new and fresh and raw and beautiful and the first step in the direction of even greater things than what was once to be. I celebrate *Wild Honey* as a work of joy, and one more gift of music from probably the most creative musician alive. I celebrate *Wild Honey* for "Country Air," for "I'd Love Just Once to See You," for "Aren't You Glad," for "Darlin' " . . . for all this music that is so listenable and so moving and so very very original and good on the level of what I believe music really is. I celebrate *Wild Honey.*

Hooray!

The Tragedy of *Smile*

November 1967 / March 1968

I.

PAUL: Why don't we start off from the— DAVID: Crying. PAUL: Crying? (laughter) DAVID: where would you like to start? PAUL: I guess we might as well start from how difficult this album makes it, and then just take it back and see what happens. DAVID: Okay. In a way, it doesn't make it as difficult as *Smiley Smile* did, because *Smiley Smile* was closer to the stuff that he cut for the original *Smile* album. PAUL: It's easier to forget this one. DAVID: Right. But you can't forget *Smiley Smile,* if you were around when Brian was cutting the stuff for the original *Smile.*

It's very hard to listen to this album, *Wild Honey,* and figure out what . . . there's so much that could cause that, it's difficult to really ascertain, not seeing Brian for a while, what it could be. The fact of his trying to cut in his own house I think has a lot to do with it, 'cause that's limiting him. I think the major problem from *Pet Sounds* to this album is, um, the fact that the Beach Boys, the Beach Boys number one as a musical instrument and the Beach Boys always being negative towards Brian's experimentation. They were generally very aware of the commercial market, when Brian really wanted to space out and take off, and would've been the first . . . "I Am the Walrus," for instance. Brian was doing Hawaiian chants, we used to lay around the house a year and a half ago, a year ago, a bunch of us, and do Hawaiian chants and all kinds of chanting, and all kinds of animal noises. Everything that's being done now that I hear, it's like old hat—it's like laying around Brian's house. But then he would go through some kind of a number waiting for the guys to return, because he knew that they would balk at that kind of experimentation at that point. They wanted to stay pretty much within the form of what the Beach Boys had created—really hard . . . whatever that is, California rock or whatever.

It's a very hard thing to explain. For instance, Brian could cut a whole album like *Pet Sounds* by himself. Which is why, I think, that Brian is really the foremost person in rock music. The ability for him to sit down, at a piano, and write a song, and take it into the studio, and not only produce it but engineer it, control the board, know exactly what he wants to do, play almost any of the instruments he wants to play, chart it himself, uh, and sing all the parts! Had he been able to do that, and do it today, you wouldn't have a *Wild Honey,* I don't think. I don't think you would have a *Smiley Smile.* You would have had the *Smile* that you heard some parts of, that are still sittin' around somewhere, that's got to be one of the great albums of all time, if it ever comes out.

Other than that, I really don't know why *Wild Honey* is there. It's so naked compared to what he has in him. And he can't lose it. A person like Brian cannot *lose* what he has.

Now maybe mentally he could be off into another thing, 'cause Brian has a tendency to get into things, you know he uh, he gets all that fantastic energy, that, uh, I don't like to use the word genius, but he gets that fantastic Brian Wilson thing into a direction and it's like, everyone watch out, it's like a tank moving through wheat, and he'll go until he gets bored. Not *tired*, 'cause Brian never gets tired, but when he gets bored immediately it's off, and he's onto another direction. I don't know what direction this is. At all. This is no direction . . . it's almost pacification, it's almost giving up. You really get a feeling that Brian is either tired, or he's given up, or he just doesn't give a shit. It could be, perhaps, that he just doesn't give a shit at this point.

PAUL: What happened to the record company, to Brother Records? DAVID: Brother Records is very close and dear to my heart. At the time that I left, or that Brian and I parted company on a business level, officially, whatever, Brother Records was just in the formation stages. Brother Records was really a dream that Brian had, a nonbusiness concept that I somehow in a series of very long conversations over a long period of time, tried to show Brian how to structure it. Hence, when it was time to get serious, my function was to be head of Brother Records, which was exactly that, either head or chief. There were no titles. It was gonna be the first real non-up-tight, positive, youth company, record company, and all our juices were directed in that direction. We were going to do things that had never been done before, there were not going to be any weirdnesses like you run into in the record business right now.

But it can't be that way. As long as you have to maintain a business that deals with the distributors, for instance, or the people who can't get on your trip, then somehow you have to compromise, and somehow you have to play a little of their game. Brian was totally uncompromising. And probably, had I been crazy enough at that time, and given Brian the total strength that I should have given to him, we could have done it, 'cause Brian can really do anything he says he's gonna do. There's just no question of that.

Well, we got Brother Records going. The first thing we had to do was sever the relationship with Capitol Records. Uh . . . Brother Records was not really formed so that the Beach Boys could make more money; Brother was formed so that Brian could have more free direction. Which doesn't look like that's happening. I mean this is the great paradox, it looks like he's tied more now than he was before. It could be the restrictions of having his own label, maybe . . . PAUL: Well, *Wild Honey* has been released on Capitol . . . DAVID: And I have no idea why that is. When I was told that *Wild Honey* was coming out on Capitol I tried to search in my head, one, what kind of an agreement they could have made . . . PAUL: Maybe Brian thinks, if it comes out on Capitol, it doesn't count. DAVID: That's very good. That's very good, 'cause Brian has a naive streak running through him which is really beautiful, and you wish you could hop onto that naive thing. Brother Records was like a precious little oasis; it was going to have only those things that Brian was in love with.

I left because at the time that *Smile* was being done, it was impossible to run Brother Records as a business. No decisions could be made. Brian at that time got his head out of the business thing completely and into the studio, and then got his head completely out of anywhere; we couldn't find where his head was at for a whole long period of time. And operating a business without being able to get decisions from Brian just wouldn't work. So I moved out. A lot of us moved out. I really don't know that much about Brother at this point, except what I see, and what I see is not really that happy.

PAUL: Let's try to trace the history of *Smile*, from *Dumb Angel* [Brian's original name for the album] or even earlier; in fact, why don't we start with the origins of *Pet Sounds*, however much you know, and just go right through? DAVID: Fine. Okay. The origins of *Pet Sounds* . . . At one point I came into the Beach Boys' lives, or into Brian's life, right around the *Beach Boys Today* and *Beach Boys Concert* albums . . . PAUL: March '65. DAVID: Right, somewhere around there—I came in through a relative of mine who was a friend of a few of the Beach Boys and then I was out again. And then I was brought up to Brian's house one night, a long time ago, and we just hung out for a while, and it was very groovy. I really liked Brian right away, I liked him because there was something there, that I had not seen in many people in my lifetime. And I was out again. The people in Brian's life are very much in and out, in and out; you're around for a while, and then you're gone, because of Brian's . . . the thing I mentioned earlier, the fact that Brian gets into something so intently and then he's out of it and he goes into a new thing, and if you personally can't get into the new thing then either you have to go by yourself or they make it known, on a very non-up-tight level, that you're just not fitting in.

When I really got in with Brian was right around the time of the fourth final "Good Vibrations." I heard it, and it knocked me out, and I said, uh oh there's something happening here that is unbelievable. And then, the next time I came up, it was different. And the next time I came up it was different. And then I came up one evening, and Brian said—at that time I had left MGM, and I was managing an artist named Danny Hutton, who is now recording for Brian— Brian informed me at that time that he had decided to totally scrap "Good Vibrations." He was not going to put it out. The track was going to be sold to Warner Brothers to be put out as an r&b song, sung by a colored group. Brian has always had a feeling for r&b, *very* heavy feeling for r&b. So I went home, I talked to Danny and Danny said, well, let's work out a deal, let's see if I can't record the song and have Brian produce it and finish it and the whole thing. I called Brian back the next day and I proposed, made a proposal to him, which I don't personally think caused him to decide to finish, but maybe he . . . it gave him a different perspective. Anyway, he went ahead and he finished it.

PAUL: What was the nature of the earlier "Good Vibrations?" DAVID: It was a lot shorter, it was a lot tighter rhythmically, melodically it was a lot simpler than the final song. It was much more a commercial ditty, if that's possible. There were no lyrics at that time, that he had recorded; he had just recorded tracks. Brian goes in and cuts all the tracks first. He is motivated by the music, generally; the music will then motivate the lyric, and a lot of times the lyric comes very late. Brian is totally musical. Obviously he's not lyrical. Brian has written some of the worst lyrics in history. Although you shouldn't say "worst" lyrics, but some of the simplest lyrics. His lyrics have never been on the par that his music has been on, ever. He really has a musical head.

PAUL: "Sloop John B." ended up an integral part of *Pet Sounds,* and really fit; but was it created before the rest of the album? DAVID: Oh yes. PAUL: I understand it was an attempt to give the Beach Boys a virile image, a masculine image. DAVID: Well, at that time they had started getting hit, the whole hippie thing had started. You remember, now the hippie thing is coming, the underground is starting to bubble up for the first time. PAUL: *Revolver.* DAVID: Right. The Beatles have done *Revolver,* uh, Dylan is popular, Dylan is a big thing, Dylan was a big thing for Brian. He had a very big thing going for Bob Dylan. He thought Bob Dylan was . . . ha, very amusingly . . . he felt that Dylan was placed in the music scene to end music. He thought that musically he was very destructive, although lyrically . . . interestingly enough, if you go back, one of the few songs that Brian has ever recorded on an album that has not been a Brian Wilson song is a Bob Dylan song, they recorded a Bob Dylan thing ["The Times They Are A-Changing"] on the *Beach Boys Party* album. PAUL: Great album. DAVID: Right! PAUL: Now there's one that will eventually get credit for being a first. DAVID: And that album has the feeling— PAUL: of the

Stones' lp. DAVID: Right, that has that whole, beautiful laying-around-the-house, doing a number . . . PAUL: And, with the musical integrity. DAVID: Way ahead of its time.

Brian was taking a great deal of slamming at that time from the heavy critics about them being, you know, "wimp-rock," and "ball-less rock," and "high school sopranoes" and the whole number. There were very few people who recognized the genius of Brian Wilson. So he wanted to get into that a little bit, and then he also got into some mind-expanding ventures that allowed him to really sit back and hear things for the first time. He himself personally was going through some changes; he became very interested in Subud, then moved on into astrology, numerology, occult . . . Brian is a fantastic reader, this is another thing people don't understand. If people would take time to talk to him—'cause he doesn't talk, he's nonverbal, he's a nonverbal human who reads intently, reads some of the heaviest material and instantly knows exactly what's going on. Somebody tried to lay the I Ching on him for a period of time—he had the whole thing psyched out, if that's possible, he had the thing psyched out immediately. Now again, his study of numerology, and Subud, and all the occult was not what you would call normal, it was so far more intent than man is supposed to go. I mean he really gets into it, to such a point that when you're with him, at five o'clock in the morning, and you're laying around and he's discussing certain things with you, that you absolutely want not to believe, he forces you to believe them, with an incredible amount of knowledge of the subject, and then a tremendous amount of perception. The most perceptive man I've ever met is Brian Wilson.

Anyway, all this was going on at the same time, this is all happening now and he's starting to meet people . . . who are not from Hawthorne, California. He's starting to meet other people who are into different areas of, uh, academic study, or intelligentsia, and they're starting to lay numbers on his head, and Brian is like eating all this up, as he always does. Then he gets into *Pet Sounds*. *Pet Sounds* was a very long project, it was the cutting of a whole bunch of tracks, which is his pattern, same pattern as *Smile*, going in and getting an idea, going in and putting it down, putting it away, doing something else, putting it down, putting it away, and then taking these pieces and getting them together; sometimes what he thought was gonna be one song in fact became another song, and what he thinks is the lead of this thing ends up being the end of another thing.

And this is when I started getting very close to Brian. I was coming up to the house all the time, and each time I came up he would lay a new track on us, and it was like unbelievable to hear this stuff happening. Umm, it was very hard to relate to. Without the words, just the music, it was like a symphony being written. PAUL: It still is. DAVID: Right, exactly . . . and I think then he started encountering his first problems with the Beach Boys. The first "No Brian, we shouldn't go this far out, why are we knocking success? Let's stay within the frame of, let's do the simple dumb thing, let's not go too far out, let's not lose what the Beach Boys are, uh, let's not change our physical image, let's wear the striped shirts and the white pants," the clean-cut image, which changed if you remember with the English recognition . . .

PAUL: Was there a ringleader on this? DAVID: Uh, no, you couldn't really say a ringleader. I think probably the most antagonistic situation was between Brian and Mike Love, although it is not an antagonistic kind of . . . They're very close, there's a great deal of love between all the fellas. I don't think any of the other boys, except perhaps for Carl, is anywhere near where Brian is musically, although Dennis showed some great moments, he was doing some of his own things and they were very beautiful. . . . But Brian would come in, and he would want to do different things, and they really would balk at that; and again, I have to keep thinking that this is the problem with what's going on right now. Sooner or later it has to tire you out, and Brian would complain about it. It would be much easier for Brian to go in and lay all those voices out himself, and do all those things; there's a lot of things on *Pet Sounds* that, uh, incredible vocal things that are all Brian's voices, 'cause he can sing all their parts.

But he would go through a tremendous paranoia before he would get into the studio, knowing he was going to have to face an argument. He would come into the studio up tight, he would give a part to one of the fellas or to a group of the fellas, say "This is what I would like to have done," and there would be resistance. And it wouldn't be happening and there would be endless takes and then he would just junk it. And then maybe after they left to go out on tour he would come back in and do it himself. All their parts. But it was very taxing, and it was extremely painful to watch. Because it was, uh, a great wall had been put down in front of creativity.

And now, maybe, he just doesn't want to fight any more. It used to·be a big fight thing in that studio, and he just may be damn well tired of fighting and having to give the parts to the guys and hearing their excuses why they don't want to do it this way or why they want to do it that way . . . that could very easily be it. Maybe he's biding his time; I don't know. I really . . . it just, uh, this is very scary. Something's gonna happen with Brian; we all know it. Those of us who've been around him know that something very quickly is gonna explode and it's gonna be beautiful, whatever it is, but I don't think it's gonna be with the Beach Boys. I would almost say for sure that the next big Brian Wilson thing will not be with the Beach Boys.

Now here's an important thing, though, which explains somewhat *Smiley Smile* and maybe *Wild Honey:* Brian, a long time ago, was incredibly interested in humor, pure, beautiful, positive humor. And if you listen to the Beatles now, and the Stones and the Airplane, and everyone else who's doing—Janis Ian, I just heard her second album, which is incredibly bad, but she has that whole number going with the wrong things and laughing and all, everyone having a good time at the session and ha ha you get to listen in. Well, Brian was into that a long time ago; he wanted to put out the first pop humor album, and we spent days and nights running around the city tape recording different sounds and different things and getting into the most incredibly humorous things. PAUL: When? DAVID: About a year ago, just before the formation of Brother Records. Hours upon hours upon hours of videotape . . . a fantastic amount of time just spent on humor. At that time, I thought myself that it was a little crazy, that you had to maintain some sort of dignity, but Brian wanted out and out humor, complete and total humor, and was not allowed to do it. A lot of us ourselves would balk at Brian, let alone the Beach Boys, saying you know look, that's never gonna happen Brian, and now we all have egg on our face 'cause everything is humor now. And I don't know this whole game about so and so obviously is influenced by so and so and so and so is influenced by, you know, the comparison game, I don't know how deep that is or even if it does exist . . . but I have not, as I said earlier I have not heard anything that is new to my ears, I have not heard . . . it's all silliness compared to what Brian really has, or had, a year ago, that is not on this latest stuff.

The thing that I would really like to get into at this point, though, is what was happening with Brian a year ago. *Pet Sounds* had been completed, "Good Vibrations" was climbing up the charts to be their first million-selling single, they had conquered England—we were getting daily phone calls from the guys, these incredible calls with stories about the three hundred photographers at EMI, the New Musical Express, they were the Number One group, they'd overtaken the Beatles, the first act to do that, the meetings between Brian and Lennon and McCartney and all these things were going on, the first recognition of Brian from the critics, from the hippies, from the underworld was starting to happen, it was all very beautiful, a very happy time. Brian then went into the studio and started *Smile*. The majority of his work was done while the guys were in England.

During this period the creative juices of Brian Wilson were at their absolute peak. We were talking about movies, television, radio, records, publications, art; all forms of communication were going to be attacked by the Brian Wilson mind. He wanted to change radio—*again,* the FM concept that is happening now, what Tom Donahue is doing in San Francisco and LA, Brian had that whole number going a long time ago. We sat for hours and hours just thinking and talking about how lousy radio was, how obviously people, particularly kids, couldn't really be that happy to hear all this garbage coming over the air, the rapid delivery of the disk jockeys, the terrible advertisements . . . Brian wanted humorous radio, he wanted everything to be positive, everything to be light and gentle, and no control, no direction, just a framework and whatever happens. The same for television. Same thing for motion pictures.

Everything Brian said, by the way, during this period of time, struck our ears, those of us who were around, as totally insane. And then he would keep it going and going, and force us to do things with him, and the second we did it, or heard it or saw it, we realized immediately that it was right. *Anything* he said was right, no matter how outlandish it seemed . . . One of the really, uh, the uniquely beautiful things about Brian was that he never had one idea that I can remember that was simple. He never had one idea that made sense. Everything was new. Every single idea he would say had no foundation anywhere, except for his head.

This is how he got into, for instance, the chanting: one night we were at the studio, and Brian didn't feel like putting down a track. We were just laying around, and he said, "Come out here, everyone." So we all went out there, not one of us a professional, and he had us making animal noises, incredible noises, directing us from the control room: "Louder." "Softer." "More expansive." "Get in closer." The whole thing. We started off very conscious of what we were doing, looking at each other and very embarrassed, and then he just drove us into it, totally. We went into the studio and listened to it; he put it with music, we listened to it again and walked out knowing that once again Brian had done it.

This was a daily routine. To have your mind blown by something Brian was coming up with. Playing instruments at the dinner table, for instance. He was going to record a record where we would just all be playing different things, spoons, and he would have everyone doing a different rhythm. He would come by and say, "Dave, this is the rhythm I want you to do," and I would do some rhythm, and then he would go to the next person. He would get maybe fifteen people there, all doing different rhythms, and then he would come and sing over them . . . nonverbal things, just these chants, and they were absolutely stupendous. And a thing that right now hurts me personally is we used to fight him on this, say "Aw come on Brian, you know, forget it, man, pass, this is not gonna happen." And now we hear things that are like bad copies of what we were doing. I think had myself and a few other people really gotten behind him, and been on his side against whoever he had to fight, it would have happened a year and a half ago.

So we're responsible, in a way I guess, for what's happening now. The Beach Boys have to be responsible in a way, all the doubters. Brian I think for the rest of his life's gonna have to fight doubters. He was very conscious of this; he said to me more than once, "Hey man, why do you fight me?" You know, "Why are you doing this?" Or things like, "God damn it, why can't I do things the way I want to, why do I always have to have resistance?" And I couldn't give him a good answer. I myself being a painter understand the artistic freedom, yet he was so far ahead at that time that I couldn't even see where it was leading. Or, let me put it this way, I always *had* to see where it was leading, whereas Brian never was concerned with where it was leading, only that it had to be done.

PAUL: Would it be fair to say that here's a guy, one of the few people outside of certain movie directors or whatever, who's really trying to work as an individual artist in the great creative tradition, but with media? And it necessitates working with other people, working with machines, working with all sorts of things that don't do just what you want them to do?

DAVID: I think that's it. As a painter it's generally me and the canvas. As a writer, it's you and the paper. Then you may have to fight censors, or editors, but since you're the editor you've eliminated that. With Brian, it was him, then it was the Beach Boys, then it was the studio, the physical problems with electronics, then it was fighting, um, at Columbia for instance when after all these months one night one of the Columbia representatives showed up and saw Brian working the knobs on the control board and said, "You can not do that. The engineers have to do that. You are not an engineer, you are not a Columbia engineer." Brian laughed at him, he thought the guy was putting him on. But the guy was serious.

This then started Brian's getting out of other people's studios—that, plus the fact that he couldn't get time when he wanted time, which could be like three in the morning, "Let's go record." Brian could work those knobs better than anyone I've ever seen, including any engineer. He would mix a lot of his things right there as they were recording, he wouldn't have to wait, he'd be adding his echo, mixing and blending right while they were performing. The whole process was Brian! If you allowed him, he could do the whole single thing; as I said earlier, it is conceivable that *Pet Sounds* could have been done as well as it is right now or perhaps even better by just one man, Brian Wilson . . . and that's a very frightening thought, an extremely frightening thought. Because you know this man's going to go into TV, you know this man's going to go into movies, and whatever else he's going to go into. He's not picking the easy way, he's not picking the personal art form, he's picking an art form that has all the restrictions of other people's involvement. There's nothing he can't learn. You tell Brian you can't do this in films because you don't understand; you can't be a director right away, you can't be a producer because you don't understand these certain elements. He laughs at you, because it's going to be a very short period of time before he knows those elements; not only will he know them academically, but he's gonna have that creative flow going on top of it, and it's gonna elevate him way past anyone else.

PAUL: When you came in at the *Beach Boys Today* time, what did you think at that time, did it come up at all that he recorded "Bull Session with the Big Daddy" as the last track on that album? Did Brian ever mention what he had in mind? What he thought he was doing? DAVID: No. Brian would spend a great deal of time talking about things that he wanted to do, and he would do some of them, but he would also do a lot of things that none of us would ever know, before he got in and did 'em. I don't know how the hell anything like that would happen with Brian. You always have the feeling that he wasn't—he wasn't that aware of what he was doing. I mean, he knew in his head what he wanted to do, but he wasn't really aware in terms of society, or in terms of rules or mores, you know, how he was functioning within that realm. PAUL: Well, he was thoroughly aware of what he was doing, but he wasn't concerned with the same aspects of it as the rest of us. DAVID: That's the big thing with Brian. Is that he's very concerned with himself, but he's not concerned with the rest of us, other than the fact that he loves to entertain the rest of us. He really has a very positive feeling about people, incredibly so. An incredible amount of humor. Always looks for the humor in a human, if he can't find humor in the human being on any level, then that human being has to be, you know, pushed away, merely because he cannot function with him, he cannot function with people who have no humor.

Another thing: his humor is a particular kind of humor. Not being exposed, not being worldly, his humor is very Hawthorne, California. So *Smiley Smile* seems to a lot of us to be really corny, terribly corny, and very "in" on a Hawthorne level. The things I can't relate to on that album are things that I feel were like high school days to me, which to Brian are not necessarily high school days. PAUL: Did you grow up out here? DAVID: Oh yeah, I was born and raised here. PAUL: 'Cause another thing, it makes it difficult for the rest of the country to even know what it was like. Because Southern California is, it seems to me to be, twice as American as any other part of America. DAVID: And the part of Southern California that Brian grew up in is *so* American, it's incredible. There's . . . I lived in a place called Inglewood, California, which is very close to Hawthorne, and what you have there is the people who came in in the thirties from Oklahoma, from the dust bowl days, and then you have a lot of people coming during the Second World War, because all the defense plants were out there. You had people coming from the Midwest to work in defense plants. So you have a tremendous amount of Midwestern culture, right there by the beach. It's kind of like Iowa with a beach, is really what it's like down there.

PAUL: It's letting go. The whole Iowa thing comes in, but loosens its belt, relaxes, so you have sort of a cross between the Midwest and the Deep South. DAVID: Yeah, there's a lot of southern influence. The one thing you don't have, is you don't have a lot of New England sophistication. Or the kind of provincial thing you get on the opposite hand in New England. You don't have any of that out here. It's really . . . and then the weather, everything in Southern California really ties in, the kind of clothes we wear, running around ten months out of the year, eleven months out of the year in the sun, a healthy physical thing. Again, another incredibly important aspect of Brian Wilson is physical health. Incredible. I could go on for hours on physical numbers we would have to go through. Brian thought we could never get anything done until we were physically able to move—then would come the head, the head would start to clear up along with the body. The swimming pool for instance with Brian was *never* thought to be a luxury. Swimming was important for physical tuning. We had a lot of business discussions right out there in the middle of the pool, because of the water gently, you know, what the water does to the body and the head. A lot of our problems were solved right out there in the pool at four o'clock in the morning when it was 28 degrees outside, standing right out there, naked as jaybirds, 92 degrees, the steam flowing up, discussing heavy business. And it worked, every time.

PAUL: Is Brian very sensitive about being referred to, as he often is, in the press, as fat? DAVID: Oh, he's got to be. Oh sure. PAUL: Is he fat, really? DAVID: I don't think he is. I know he's strong as an ox. He's a fantastic athlete, very proud of the fact that he's a great athlete, good baseball player, football player, basketball, whatever. If you remember, in looking at the pictures of the Beach Boys on their first couple of albums, Brian was always very tall and skinny. Not even was he well built, but he was very thin. So it's got to hurt him. And I don't understand why people call him fat; that really is not important, except that he needs that, he needs the energy that that kind of weight puts on, to carry his mind. His mind is always working so fast and so much that if he didn't have that bulk, he wouldn't make it.

PAUL: Well, why people do it is that they're creating this whole Southern California, Beach Boy myth . . . DAVID: I guess the same way they talk about Dennis's muscles, 'cause he's so muscular. PAUL: And it's something that tends to offend people, you know, when the group comes on stage. People are most of all offended by the Beach Boys on stage, or were . . . DAVID: By chubby little Carl, and— PAUL: And the way Mike Love carried on, and then everything just seemed to . . . DAVID: And the clothes, the striped shirts and the white buck shoes, and the slacks and the whole thing. They're not like that offstage, that was the great paradox, is that they in their own ways were as hip as anyone I've ever met. I know that they always used to talk about Brian wearing striped shirts, the striped surfer shirts offstage and the white pants and all, that's groovy, I mean what does that have to do with the whole number? Other than the fact that yes he is presenting himself, he is what he is and he's presenting himself physically. I guess if he wore a cape they'd be a lot happier.

II.

PAUL: Let's try to take it historically . . . some of the development of *Pet Sounds* we got into, some we didn't. You know, starting from "Sloop John B," what came, what got built, to the point that it finally became a whole album, and what he started out thinking of the album as, what he ended up thinking of it as, and then the transition from that into *Smile* . . . DAVID: Well, the first thing Brian will come up with is a concept, an album concept; generally he wants to do a thing. I say "a thing" because it's, you don't really know what it is, he throws out a whole bunch of words at you, one-liners, and words and half-phrases, and you really don't know what he's talking about at all. All you know is to go along with it. The Beach Boys could walk into a session and not have the slightest idea what they're recording that night. He tells them what to record, and they do it. They don't know what it means, generally, and that was always a problem too. We're gonna do a piece of this, and a piece of that, a fragment, and they would do it, as instruments.

So with *Pet Sounds, Pet Sounds* to my knowledge was never *Pet Sounds* until the end, it was just things he was recording. He would get a musical idea. He would then extend off that musical idea. In doing that extension, something else would pop up. So he would stop the first thing and then take off on the second thing. He would develop the new concept that hit his head, until he came to another concept. He would then abandon for a while that second thing and start off on the third, so that what he was doing was building, like with blocks or a web; that's why there was the beautiful consistency within *Pet Sounds,* musically. His things tie together so tight because, as I said earlier, what is at one time the first song, may later be part of the sixth.

And then the lyrics started happening, at the same time. He may get into a feeling on one thing. He'll play, he'll hear a track, and he'll say gee this track is a beautiful thing to express a feeling between a guy and a girl, or this one should be a relationship between this and this. Then he'll start to do the words on it. Then it becomes a song, and then it gets a title, the titles really don't mean anything, I sometimes don't think the words mean anything in certain places. But that's how he builds an album, that's how *Pet Sounds* came about.

PAUL: Did the beginnings of work on *Pet Sounds* coincide with his decision to stop traveling with the group? DAVID: Definitely. It was also the beginning of his sound effects, which in a way was the beginning of sound effects in pop music, on the level that it is now. *Pet Sounds* is directly related to the last little track with the train and the two dogs, the two dogs are his dogs, they are family to him. He was very happy with *Pet Sounds.* Extremely happy with that album, thought that he had done something very important, and was very unhappy that it didn't do well commercially, for the first time he was aware of that. But he'd experimented himself, and succeeded. So therefore when it was time to get into *Smile,* the initial involvement into *Smile* . . .

It was just impossible to keep up with that man. He was setting up blocks of studio time, would get up tight if he couldn't get a studio at four . . . four in the morning he'd be sitting around and he'd get an idea and he'd want to be able to go in the next morning, like at seven or eight, and record. Couldn't do that, obviously, because you can't operate that way. Again, one of the restrictions . . . But his whole attitude towards *Smile* was another extension of *Pet Sounds*. Certain things had happened in *Pet Sounds* for him, for the first time, and he really wanted to get that *Smile*. It was going to be a monument. That's the way we talked about it, as a monument.

Brian got in with Van Dyke Parks at this time. PAUL: How did that happen? DAVID: I'm not sure really how that happened. My involvement with Brian when Van Dyke entered the picture was still on a very social level; I remember one night talking to someone, and someone said Van Dyke has been up to Brian's house and they're gonna work together. And I thought, Wow! Man, that's gonna be unbelievable. And I was perplexed as to how the two of them came together. PAUL: Was Michael Vosse in the picture at this time? DAVID: Michael was just starting to get into the picture. Paul Robbins was starting to get into the picture at this time. Then when I started coming up to the house a whole bunch, when the Brother Records thing started to happen, Van was there like all the time. And Van and Brian were running together, very hot and heavy. And Van was blowing Brian's mind, and Brian was blowing Van's mind. And I looked at the whole situation and I said, at that time, that's never going to work. Those two are never gonna be able to work together.

And they never have, they never really did. They had a great moment of creativity. I think Van Dyke is one of the few, very few people that Brian truly looked at on an equal level, or maybe that's a little presumptuous to say. Van Dyke blew Brian's mind and I hadn't seen anyone else do that. And Van used to walk away, from his evenings with Brian, very awestruck at what Brian was doing musically. I think to this day Van Dyke is the first one to admit—again, not influence but the effect that Brian had, or has, on Van Dyke.

Very strong. Their parting was kind of tragic, in the fact that there were two people who absolutely did not want to separate but they both knew that they had to separate, that they could not work together. 'Cause they were too strong, you know, in their own areas. PAUL: When, February? DAVID: Right around February, yeah. Van was getting—his lyric was too sophisticated, and in some areas Brian's music was not sophisticated enough, and so they started clashing on that. PAUL: They missed each other. DAVID: Yeah. They were together to a certain point, and then zingo! they bypassed each other, and never the twain shall meet with those two.

PAUL: Let's try to remember the tracks. "The Elements" . . . DAVID: Okay. *Smile* was going to be the culmination of all of Brian's intellectual occupations; and he was really into the elements. He ran up to Big Sur for a week, just 'cause he wanted to get into that, up to the mountains, into the snow, down to the beach, out to the pool, out at night, running around, to water fountains, to a lot of water, the sky, the whole thing was this fantastic amount of awareness of his surroundings. So the obvious thing was to do something that would cover the physical surroundings.

We were aware, he made us aware, of what fire was going to be, and what water was going to be; we had some idea of air. That was where it stopped. None of us had any ideas as to how it was going to tie together, except that it appeared to us to be an opera. And the story of the fire part I guess is pretty well known by now. PAUL: There's a lot of confusion about it. DAVID: Well, briefly, Brian created a track for the fire part which was the most revolutionary sound I've ever heard. He actually created a fire, a forest fire, with instruments, no sound effects—a lot of strings, and a lot of technique on the board—when you would listen to that thing it would actually, it would scare you, you would be scared listening to that. It was so overpowering . . . and then there was a rash of fires in the city, and Brian became very aware of this rash of fires, and then there was the fire across the

street from the studio . . . Brian's not superstitious, he's something that I can't name, 'cause I totally do not understand
what it is, but he had a series of dialogues with me where at
one point he asked if I would check the fire department, call
the city fire department or whoever it was that I would have
to call, to find out if there were more fires within this period
in Los Angeles than in any other period in history. Because
he really felt, I guess the word is vibrations. Brian is very
into vibrations, and made me, to this day, very aware of
vibrations. Anyway, after we all laughed at him, as we
normally did in these situations, he went ahead and destroyed
the tape. Completely. Eliminated it, never to be heard again.
That basically destroyed "Elements."

PAUL: Was this the first break in *Smile,* the first turn down-
ward? DAVID: Yeah. That was the first sign that we were going to have problems on this album. That, and the fact that
for the first time Brian was having trouble with studios—
getting studio time. Then he was having a problem with
engineers. Brian was starting to meet a fantastic amount of
resistance on all fronts. Like, very slowly everything started
to collapse about him. The scene with Van Dyke. Now, that's
a critical point. You've gotta remember that originally Van
Dyke was gonna do all the lyrics for *Smile.* Then there was
a hassle between Van and Brian and Van wasn't around.
So that meant that Brian was now going to have to finish
some of the lyrics himself. Well, how was he gonna put his
lyrics in with the lyrics already started by Van Dyke? So
he stopped recording for a while. Got completely away from
music, saying, it's time to get into films. And we all knew
what was happening.

So he abandoned the studio. Then, there was the business,
Brother Records. He got his head into the business aspects
of Brother Records. So that kept him out of . . . he had another excuse. Then there was the attention. David Oppen-
heim coming into town to do the Leonard Bernstein special
on pop, and there was that whole number going on. And this

guy coming up from that paper, and you yourself came up, and a lot of people started coming, people that Brian had never met before, *kinds* of people that Brian had never met before. So he was spending a lot of his time questioning me as to the validity of critics, the importance of certain people, why is it important that all of a sudden they're doing this, and all the time knowing that it was important, but not being able, because he'd not been exposed in the past, not being able to tell who was real and who was not real. There was gonna be the *Post* article by Jules Siegel, he was on television, an incredible amount of excuses not to cut, things to get into. The little film for "Good Vibrations," which took time away; the guys being out of town, whatever, he was clinging onto excuses.

And I was very aware of what was happening, but I couldn't put my finger onto why *Smile* was now starting to nose-dive, other than the fact that I still felt at that point that the central thing was Van Dyke's severing of that relationship. PAUL: The creative period had been passed and the specific concept was beginning to slip away. DAVID: Right. What had happened was, Brian had gone in and had done a fantastic amount of recording while the guys were in Europe, and then there was a separation of time, and then it got to be, well, as soon as they get back we'll finish. And they got back. And they had their normal rest time. And then he brought them into the studio, and they were hearing things they never heard before. Not only were they hearing things they'd never heard from Brian, but you've got to remember that none of this Beatles stuff was happening then. There was no way to relate to what Brian was putting down.

That's when he started meeting resistance from the Beach Boys. "Brian, what are you . . . what is this? What are you doing? This is not within our framework, you're going too far now Brian, this is too experimental. I can't sing this part." In one specific song Brian wanted to sing the lead, but it was almost promised to Mike. And Mike couldn't cut it the way

Brian wanted it to be cut, although Mike was cutting it beautifully. But it still wasn't right, and Brian wanted to do it . . . they went through an incredible amount of time, almost a whole week of wasted studio time, before Brian finally did it.

Brian didn't know how to deal with the boys. We were around for the first time; the Beach Boys came back from England and here was this bunch of people, who all of a sudden were saying a lot of things—Michael Vosse, and myself, and Paul Robbins somewhat, Van Dyke, very strongly, Jules, a lot of people they hadn't seen before—and that must have been very scary for them, 'cause here was a whole bunch of people who were doing heavy things for their career, their future. And here's Brian, with entirely new sounds. I think had they relaxed into *Smile, Smile* would have happened. 'Cause you've got to remember, to this day *Smile* is still an album of tracks that are filed away somewhere, not many vocals down, but there's still a whole album—there's enough there for three albums of incredible tracks.

"Heroes & Villains" was a critical track on the album. Would have been a critical part of *Smile* in its original form, not in the form that came out. Now here's another thing that happened. Now he's involved with the lawyers. Now he's involved with Capitol Records, and we're into a lawsuit, we're into a very big lawsuit . . . How do we get into a lawsuit and still maintain our positive image? We cannot be the villains, remember; we've got to be the heroes, at all times. We cannot be bad guys. All right Brian, he was told one day, at this point in order for us to get what we have to get for Brother Records, we've got to have a single out. That old, lousy thing that still exists in our business: you've got to have the single out. There's always a reason. Whether it's for the lawsuit, or because your image is failing, or you haven't had one out in five months, or the last one trailed off, or the last one was a million-seller, whatever, there's always that lousy you've-got-to-have-your-single.

So Brian is told that he's got to have a single. I told Brian he had to have a single. It was the hardest thing I ever did. Brian was not at those meetings with the Capitol people. I was there. And I was in the meetings with the lawyers. Brian was not there. Nick Grillo and I would have to go to these situations, and then relate them back to Brian. It was very difficult for me to do, because I was on Brian's side. Yet, he wanted Brother Records, and I had to do the Brother Records thing and that really started to kill the creativity that was happening in *Smile*. He was getting very up tight, he was getting disappointed, he was getting disappointed in me, because now I was being business and I wasn't being, you know, I wasn't hanging out with Brian at night any more, because I had to be in an office in the morning, there was none of the five o'clock in the morning sillinesses that we used to go through. There was now calling up Brian, instead of saying let's hang out, it was Hey Brian you've got to give me an answer to something blah blah blah blah you know business, business. All this was in the framework of the fact that a normal business meeting with Brian Wilson usually meant going up to Brian's about one in the morning, going into the tent, getting it on, getting out our pieces of paper and pencils, and sitting there, and he would say okay, now: here's the structure for the business. And it would be: Number one, health. Number two, foods. Then we'd list a, b, and c, health foods. Number three, swimming. Charts. Maps. He wanted anatomy charts all over the place. Awareness of surroundings, awareness of health and all of this.

All of a sudden that was gone. Now it was, uh, Brian, we can go for half a million dollars, we can go for a million dollars blah blah. And all this was happening to him. He had to get out of the creative thing. It was just an absolute must. So that when I left, "Heroes & Villains" was being planned to be a single, only because it was the closest thing to being finished, at that point, and sadly not even the original "Heroes & Villains" because right at that time *Sergeant Pepper* came

out. PAUL: When I was there in December, Brian was thinking of "Heroes & Villains" as the single. DAVID: Right. He
would think of "Heroes & Villains," and then he would call
up two nights later and say it was going to be this, and it
was going to be that, and it was going to be "Heroes &
Villains" again, and then everyone said, No, Brian, it should
be "Heroes & Villains," no Brian it should be this . . . See,
people should never be allowed to say "No" to Brian Wilson.
Brian is a person that never should be said no to. 'Cause if
you just get behind him, or next to him, and go with him,
it's gonna come out okay.

But he was forced into that. And maybe that's why what's
happening now is happening. He probably hasn't recovered
from that. It was a big shock for him. It's like taking a person, exposing him to something he's always wanted to be in,
taking him right to the brink of it, and leaving. And saying,
"Geez Brian, how come you haven't followed up with that
whole thing? Why have you fallen down?" He zoomed right
up there, alienated from a lot of things that had been his
strengths in the past. Those strengths were ripped away,
shown to be shallow and phony, taken away from him . . .
but no foundation put under him. And the foundation that
we all had, that we were trying to supply him with, was us!
And when we went, there was nothing left there. Just him,
hanging . . . and, um, perhaps we should have never gone
in the first place. I don't know what his development would've
been; I don't think he would've gotten into some of those
things on *Smile*, though, had he not been exposed to this
whole new thing . . .   ˙

And he's gonna recover. But *Smile* . . . I don't know, I
don't even know how many tracks he finished, or worked on:
there's "The Elements," "Heroes & Villains," um . . . "Surf's
Up," which is a masterpiece, unbelievable . . . that was the
one song, "Surf's Up" was the one perfect blending of Van
Dyke and Brian. Absolute perfection. One of the most important songs I've ever heard in my life. I don't know if it

will ever be out. Let's see, what else is there . . . PAUL:
"The Child Is the Father of the Man." DAVID: Which I understand will be on his next album. I just heard that from
someone, I don't remember who told me . . . A couple of
Indian things, "Bicycle Rider." PAUL: Wasn't that part of
"Heroes & Villains"? DAVID: At one time. It was also part of
something else. Um . . . "Vegetables." PAUL: How was that
going to be? DAVID: Not like it is on the album. It's on
Smiley Smile, it was changed quite a bit. See, all that stuff
was changed, because Brian . . . none of the *tracks* are on
Smiley Smile. Some of the songs are there, but he's recorded
them in the house. "Heroes & Villains," yes, some of the
tracks were from the original. Ah . . . he was forced to put
"Good Vibrations" on, something he never wanted to do is
put a single onto the album, but he was forced to do that.
For sales. That was another, I'm sure, a minor tragedy for
him.

I think what Brian tried to do with *Smiley Smile* is he tried
to salvage as much of *Smile* as he could and at the same time
immediately go into his humor album. 'Cause it's so—I hear
elements in that of our discussions about the humor album,
just little pieces of it. PAUL: "Little Pad" is really nice. DAVID:
Yeah. Right. But you can see that there's a man straining
when he makes that album; you can see that there's a man not
caring when you hear *Wild Honey.* PAUL: Yeah. "Heroes &
Villains" is beautiful the way it came out, in a certain sense
. . . the point where it turns upside down, from animate to
inanimate, from the voices to the organ . . . but the mix
isn't quite as it should be, it sounds harsh to the ear . . .
DAVID: That's another thing that is a key indication, is that
Brian's mixing on the last two albums is nowhere near what
it was on *Pet Sounds* . . . you can tell on *Pet Sounds* there's
a man who really cared a lot about mixing, as he did on a lot
of his other things. You don't get that feeling any more.

I don't know what the relationship between Brian and the
boys is at this point, 'cause I haven't been around, but that's

gotta be affected, that's gotta be a cause of what we're hearing now. During *Pet Sounds* it was at a very good point. It was never really at a good point during *Smile*. A lot of problems, a lot of internal problems, again, because of Brother Records, because of the newness of what he was doing, their new position in the music world. Derek was around at that time . . .

PAUL: I'd like to talk about Derek. DAVID: Okay; one of my favorite all-time people. Derek Taylor I think is singly responsible for what happened in England, if nothing more than by exposing them, to England, to the right people, getting them and the Beatles together, and then getting that into the proper papers, that they were getting together. Co-ordinating the people who were getting to Brian. The English thing was Derek's. Derek's relationship with Brian was at first very strong, then went through a tremendous nose dive; they both decided to sever relationships, then they came back again, and they worked well for a while, got along very well with the other boys, and then it nosed off again, into another direction.

Brian always felt that the Beach Boys were always number two with Derek, the Beatles were always number one. He had a very strong feeling about that. And uh . . . it's a silly thing I think in a way, but at the same time totally understandable. Belonging to a record label, you see that with your own artists on the label, when one act is hot the other ones always get that paranoia, "you care more about them," you know, and it's very silly but at the same time it's an ego thing and ego things do exist, and you can't fight 'em. PAUL: That's true, and it comes from fear. DAVID: Right. But Derek did a magnificent job with the Beach Boys, I mean he did a superb job . . . they were known at that time as the faceless monsters, and he made personalities out of them.

PAUL: We talked a little about Brian's view of the world and an obvious thematic thing that we've been into is the relationship between him and the rest of the world, mostly in layers—the immediate people around him, the business world, the music business, a little further out the audience . . . The basic problem we're faced with is a great concept and a man who is capable of actually administrating that concept, and yet it did not happen. DAVID: I think the easiest way to get into this is to understand first of all that Brian is tremendously compulsive on all levels . . . and the compulsive pattern is most apparent in his relationship to individuals. You can always tell how effective a relationship is in the fact that Brian will try to show you he's ignoring something that has happened. If somebody says something that you know has hurt Brian, his immediate reaction will be to slough it off, it doesn't bother me. And you really think that it doesn't bother him, but then you'll notice that for three days he hasn't been in the studio, or for two days he hasn't smiled —you'll start noticing there are certain things about him that aren't happening. If he were having trouble with a musical idea in his head, and he got in a fight with Marilyn, the two of 'em would, it would be like a volcano. It was always that his problems with his music were one part of a combustible formula for an explosion, and anything that would happen around that would be the oxygen, let's say, and his was the fuel, and it would explode. And it would generally explode in the manner that he would become useless in terms of musical effectiveness, he would be totally useless for a great period of time.

Brian cannot go into a session with something happening in the back of his head and put that back there and hold it there and do his work. His life is his work and if he has an argument with his father at twelve o'clock in the afternoon, and it's sufficient enough argument to cause him to worry or to grieve, he's not going to be able to cut at twelve o'clock midnight. He's not going to be able to do anything effective on an artistic level until he gets that problem resolved in his head or his heart, wherever it has struck him. And the same thing with the boys, with the brothers and Mike Love, or strangers, me, Michael Vosse, whoever. Whoever would come around . . . a writer, would come up, say something wrong, strike him wrong; he'd be upset for a couple of days. Those two days were lost. He would try, he would try almost heroically to get something done, but he couldn't. It would just be like terror, it would be a lot of wasted time running around doing this, running around doing that, let's start working on the comedy album, let's go out and record water fountains, let's go out and, for instance, one night he wanted us to go into a bar and start a fight. So he could record it. And that's really carrying something pretty far.

PAUL: That's a really good example of what I was just thinking, namely that here you have a man, a really brilliant man, so that, theoretically, whatever it takes to get whatever he wants to do done is worthwhile. But to what extent is it humanly possible, for however many people it takes, to completely, for an extended period of time, go on another person's trip, and be off or just not functioning when he can't function, and be ready to go the minute—seven o'clock in the morning in the studio, whatever—that he wants to . . . to what extent is it necessary, to what extent is it possible for the people around somebody like Brian to do this? DAVID: That's one of the best questions I've ever been asked in terms of Brian Wilson, 'cause that is the heart of a relationship with Brian. To answer one part of that question, it is absolutely necessary, if you're related on any level with Brian Wilson, to be in that position, to be ready at moment's call to get out of bed and go up to the house and rap, not because he's doing it on an ego level, not because he wants to know that he's king in your part of the court, but because he needs it. And he can't find it with anyone except you at that moment.

Now, on the other hand, who can do that? Certainly I couldn't, 'cause I'm not there any more; Michael Vosse couldn't, 'cause he's not there any more, all those people couldn't, 'cause none of 'em are around any more. It's impossible—unless you have the metabolism of Brian Wilson, you can't stay on his trip. And to be related with Brian Wilson is to be on Brian Wilson's trip. You will never be with Brian Wilson on your trip, you'll always be on his trip. Because he's an artist, and he demands that. And if you don't want to be on his trip, then you pass. We all have our little things, I guess; we all have people around who travel on our trips individually; his trip is just a fantasy, that's the whole beauty of Brian's trip, is that it's an absolute fantasy, it's like living Disneyland. There's no way to relate to it at all. PAUL: True creativity . . . the ability to make something up out of nothing. DAVID: Continually! And each thing more fantastic than the one previous! PAUL: Steady state theory of the universe. DAVID: Right.

There is one fellow who is around, who's been around for a long time with Brian, who has been able to stay on his trip, a kid named Arnie Geller, who should never be taken lightly. Arnie is Boswell to Brian's Johnson. He's a very important person in Brian's life; he is the person who will always be there. And because of that, he allows Brian to get things done. If there's no one around, when Brian needs someone, I don't think Brian can get that much done. Except writing. He needs no one for his music. Just him for his music. But to function as a human, he needs company, he needs people. Arnie . . . Arnie is the one who designed the cover for *Wild Honey,* he is basically an artist. His function is as an artist, graphic artist; I imagine he, at this point, is also Brian's contact with the office, with Brother Records, with Nick Grillo, who runs the office for the Beach Boys, he runs all their functions for them . . . Uh, I don't like to say Arnie is Brian's man, because that's like degrading him, and he shouldn't be degraded. He's his partner. He's his comrade. He's his friend.

Another one who's close is Steve Korthof, who is a relative of the Beach Boys; businesswise, he's, for lack of a better word, a band boy, but he's not their band boy, he's more than that. Again, he's a friend. He's a confidant. He is a solid foundation in their whole thing. He's one of the most beautiful people I've ever known. And very important in the Beach Boys picture, very important in Brian Wilson's picture. He travels with the guys, on the road. Takes care of the equipment. Watches the sound. Takes care of their personal problems. But not in terms of, "Hey, Steve, run down and get me a Coke." He's not a go-for. Dennis is having problems, Steve goes to Dennis's room and raps with him, gets him out of his problem. One of the guys doesn't want to do something, Steve is the one who's sent. Then when he's in town, he always happens to find his way up to Brian's house at very critical moments. He's foundation. He's physically strong, morally strong, and something that Brian can always relate to; one of the few people Brian can always relate to in any dangerous situation. He knows he can always get Steve, and Steve will get it done. Steve will take care of the situation. And when you're as volatile as Brian Wilson is, you need that. Without Steve and Arnie I think Brian wouldn't even be able to do the albums he's doing now. He'd be totally ineffectual, in terms of moving around the outside world.

. . . Marilyn, is a saint! Marilyn is unbelievable. Marilyn is the perfect artist's wife, or lover, or mate; she's everything. She puts up—obviously—with the most incredible, impossible scenes I have ever been involved in; she puts up with a man who at one time is a raving lunatic, to another moment, an absolute saint, himself. You know, that tremendous paradox of personalities. They fight, and they love. She's always there. There's a great feeling I get from being close to both of them, there's a great feeling of love. That's his tangible man-woman love, Marilyn. She can be the mistress of the home, 'cause Brian likes to entertain; but Brian does not entertain like anyone I've ever seen entertain. Brian can have a dinner, which he did lots of times, a dinner for a lot of people, which for two days ahead of time he's incredibly excited about; gets the people up to the house that he wants up to the house; and then won't show for dinner. In the middle of dinner he'll run in maybe and wolf down the food in three seconds and he's gone again. She keeps that whole thing together. When Brian gets into his very deep depressions, Marilyn is the only one I've ever seen able to really get to him. She's a very beautiful person; very simple, very plain, exactly what he needs. Very, very groovy.

PAUL: Is there a song that's, particularly— DAVID: For her? I couldn't say. I don't know. See, you never know with him, he doesn't give you those clues. Brian doesn't make his work obvious, like a lot of writers. Brian is absolutely unpretentious as an artist. He just is not aware of creating things, images and symbols and creating a life and taking advantage of the position he's in. So you never know with Brian, he just goes, he just does his thing. And you really never know exactly what that thing is.

There's a strong mother and father thing happening with Brian; sometimes it's very negative, sometimes it's very positive. Extreme in both cases. I mean, it's not a normal son/parent relationship, it's a very active relationship between family. Extremely close to the mother, and very tight bond between father and son. Also a competition between father and son, that sometimes gets very sticky. I don't think fathers and sons should be in competition. . . . A factor that affects Brian's creativity. A bad note from the father or a bad scene with the father can affect Brian for weeks, days; in the same way, a good thing with his father can put him in a state of exhilaration. Exaltation. So it's very critical at that point.

. . . Dennis. Dennis is the kind of person that will ask you to go shopping with him, and whatever he buys for himself he'll buy for you. That's Dennis. He will go out to get a motorcycle, and if you're with him, he'll buy you a motorcycle. Incredibly . . . always on edge, completely on edge, you never know with Dennis at any second whether he's gonna explode or not. No matter whether he's happy or sad.

He is completely free, an animal, a free animal . . . who is almost always controlled by his emotions, and very seldom by his head. A beautiful younger brother, and one that Brian can really relate to—a very easy brother relationship for Brian to relate to and also a source of incredible enjoyment for Brian. Brian would spend a great deal of time talking about Dennis, just going into big raps about Dennis. Apparently the easiest one of all for Brian to understand. He still has a physical thing that Brian can relate to, the strength, the athletic ability, the whole thing. PAUL: Surfing came from Dennis. DAVID: Right. Hot rods. PAUL: The enthusiasm. DAVID: Dennis. Always Dennis. Even the love of outdoors. But here's the interesting thing. All the fantasies Brian would get, Dennis would take even farther. In other words, Brian would come up with the ideas, but once he would lay them on Dennis's head, they were gone. I mean, Dennis would shoot 'em right to the extreme. Brian would say it would really be groovy if everyone got into the ocean, Dennis would buy a boat. Brian would still talk about the ocean, or he'd rent a boat and go out. If Brian said, "God, it would be great to have motorcycles," Dennis would have a motorcycle outfit, a motorcycle, and would be doing the most incredible mountain-climbing numbers you've ever seen. That's Dennis.

And Carl is the spirit. Brian goes to Carl for the spiritual thing. Brian feels that Carl is the most spiritual person he's ever personally known. And perhaps he is; I don't know. There's a certain something . . . the vibration thing is Carl. Brian is deeply, emotionally involved with Carl. On a very, very heavy level. PAUL: Is Carl the youngest brother? DAVID: Yeah. PAUL: Are there only the three? DAVID: Yeah, there's the three brothers and then Mike Love, who's a cousin. PAUL: Is there a sister? DAVID: No. That's the family.

PAUL: What does the brother thing have to do with the group? DAVID: The brother thing is obviously very strong, in the fact that Brian is still producing the Beach Boys, when as I said earlier it would be much easier for him to produce himself. That's the Beach Boys. They're always my brothers and then the Beach Boys. Always my brothers first. The whole Beach Boy mystique, the Beach Boy thing, the thing that I used to get a great deal of personal fun out of, is when people would arbitrarily slough off or slam the Beach Boys as being wimp, or whatever they wanted to call 'em, they really had no idea of the incredible complex thing that is happening amongst a group of people. You could do a trilogy just on the lives of the Beach Boys. There is so much emotion, and drama, in that family, much more than I've ever seen in any other family, and everything directly affects Brian. Brian is always conscious of those boys, continually conscious of them, as brothers and as human beings. Very seldom as an act.

Again, that's why, a great reason why *Smile* wasn't finished, the way Brian wanted it, because of their resistance in the studio. PAUL: And one way of finishing it would have been to break up the group. But he didn't do that. DAVID: Which he talked about. On many occasions. But it was easier, I think, to get rid of the outsiders like myself than it was to break up the brothers. You can't break up brothers.

. . . Mike Love? Businessman. Continually being accused by Brian of being mercenary, soulless—very untrue, Mike is a very soulful person. He's the only one really who is aware of business, for the group. At the same time Michael is the one who has opposed experimentation stronger than anyone else. He's the one more divorced of the family relationship in the group. Brian's opposite number, you know, he's the one who is continually fighting Brian, the hardest one for Brian to control, the hardest one for Brian to deal with; and I've seen Mike send Brian right out of sessions, because Brian will get so frustrated in terms of trying to relate to Mike, and not being able to. Brian will just stomp right out, and there's some more lost time, more lost creative time. Mike was the easiest one for me to relate to, outside of Brian. I had a very simple time with Mike, because Mike understood what I was trying to do on a business level.

PAUL: When *Wild Honey* does not make the top fifty albums [blush. It did. It made it to thirty], will this bring some kind of realization down on their heads? DAVID: They realize it now, they realize it *right* now. They realized it when "Heroes & Villains" didn't get higher than it did, coming off of "Good Vibrations." They realized it when *Smiley Smile* bombed. They realize it now that "Wild Honey," the single, has never been played on the radio in LA, where they're born, where they're from . . . PAUL: What do they realize? That Brian has to be set free? Or just that . . . DAVID: That something is wrong.

Brian knows, I'm sure Brian knows what's wrong. PAUL: He might even be afraid, of what it really is, because it's an ego trip, eventually, and we're all afraid of ego trips. DAVID: I think Brian is probably saying to himself a little bit, "I should have taken the other course. I should have gone ahead the way I was going to go ahead and abandoned the Beach Boys." He's gotta be thinking of that sometimes. Because he was peaking, at one point, and then it came down. They may be thinking that he *is* experimenting, although listening to *Wild Honey* there's certainly no experimentation on that album, at all.

I mean, how could a group drop as quickly as they've dropped, when they've been around so long? This isn't Question Mark and the Mysterians. PAUL: It's a time problem, there's a time problem: I'll tell you the answer to that one, because you're too close to it to see. They've only had two singles in the top ten in the last two years. Think about that. Two years! There is a turnover in the rock and roll audience of more than 50 percent in two years. And the people they've alienated have been their old-time audience, and they haven't picked up their new audience yet . . . DAVID: Well, you're right. The problem . . . you're right, though, the problem is they alienated their old-time audience with *Pet Sounds*. *Pet Sounds* was the first Beach Boy album not to be a million-seller, not to zoom right up there. They lost the teenyboppers, but they gained the other, you know, the underground, or whatever tag you want to put . . . PAUL: They *started* to, they only barely started to. DAVID: They got us, they put hooks in us . . . PAUL: Yeah, but still you run into more people than you can believe who just don't know about the Beach Boys, who should. DAVID: Well, the thing I was going to say was the ones that they hooked, they immediately lost, with the release of "Heroes & Villains," then with the album. PAUL: *Smiley Smile* was good, but it was a disappointment.

DAVID: Mmm. They're in desperate trouble right now, and it's got to be affecting Brian, and the sad thing is, for me personally, and this is why I'm very happy to be talking to you, is all those I-told-you-so's are able to say I told you so at this point, the San Francisco crowd, who called the Beach Boys at one time the California Hypes. Umm . . . All the other people who have said, "What a hype job that is," and my concern at this point is that Brian does what I know he has, you know, does his thing. PAUL: That he pull it back together. DAVID: It's there, it's there, and he's the giant, he really is the giant. And if something doesn't happen soon, he may completely abandon the whole situation.

III.

[Three months have passed since the first segments of this discussion were recorded.] DAVID: I really didn't get into the *Wild Honey* album until *John Wesley Harding* came out and everybody started saying, "Dylan has told 'em what to do, he's leading the way again, he's told everyone to go back to simplicity and forget wild production albums and just put it right where it's at." And all of a sudden I realized that once again Brian had been first.

That's exactly what *Wild Honey* is, man, that's just what it is. It's getting right back to simplicity and right back to music. And forget about how weird you can get, on an album. To me, anyway . . . that's exactly what it says to me. That, plus the fact that it's really Brian doing what he's always wanted to do. I remember when he first wrote "Surf's Up" and everybody was so excited when it was just him and the piano, and it was at that point that you could . . . if you were around at that time, you really understood where Brian's musical head was at. That same kind of need, and pleading, and his incredible loneliness were all expressed in *Wild Honey,* that kind of soul singing that he's doing. So yeah, *Wild Honey* is very groovy.

PAUL: I think the . . . the step that's been made by a number of people recently—Dylan, Brian, whoever—is not exactly a step towards simplicity—maybe some kind of artistic consciousness—the thing is, it has to include the Love album, and the Byrds album, which are obviously the same thing but which aren't "simple," on that level. DAVID: No, well, when I speak of simplicity I'm thinking in terms of what we are always told is the true art form, which is simplicity. It's not necessarily something that is simple, as such, or dumb, those are not the things that I think of . . . it's an elimination of all those things that are not necessary to make your statement. Or, um, synthesizing everything. PAUL: Yeah, making it into a unity, a monolith. DAVID: Exactly, and that's what *Wild Honey* is.

I still have to think about *Smile* a lot, that stuff that you and I heard was very complex, on many levels. But Brian was never, Brian is never complex in terms of his music—he's a complex personality, of course, but he's . . . Everything with Brian is direct and forceful and the quickest way it can get said, and again, this is *Wild Honey.* It is to me. I remember so many things that went on when I was around Brian, now when I listen to *Wild Honey,* so many things that he said, so many things that he did, and now I'm really anxious to hear the next one. I'm *really* anxious to hear his next album.

PAUL: What I feel about *Wild Honey,* and our reaction to it, is that rock had been building up to a peak of achievement on a certain level, we'd gone about as far as we could go from a given premise, which means *Wild Honey* and the Dylan album and all can be seen as some sort of breakthrough. And when that happens, whenever we emerge newborn on a higher level and we have to be small all over again, and beginning to grow—well, we get confused, we get uncertain; for a moment we feel that this new stuff has no merit at all—and it doesn't, by the old standards. 'Cause we're in a whole new place, we're dealing in new basics instead of the incredible complexities that had grown out of the old basics. The transition from *Sergeant Pepper* to *Wild Honey* is kind of like the New Year's Eve cartoons of the old man and the baby . . .

DAVID: Yeah. I think the first indication of how absurd the musical thing was getting, in terms of what we're talking about now, was "A Day in the Life." When Lennon would get into the instrumental thing, that fantastic driving until all of a sudden you realize that this is a piece of plastic or this is a piece of music and you can't explode out and disappear, no matter how many instruments you put on something, no matter what you do with the board. And I think then "I Am the Walrus" was another extreme case, to me that was extreme absurdity—and where do you go from there, and why do you have to go there? Except as a trip maybe . . . But that's not the answer, I think Brian knows that, and I think Dylan knows that . . . If "Lady Madonna" is any indication of what we have coming from the Beatles, I think now they know it too, and once again the Beatles are listening to the Beach Boys—as they always have.

I think the simpler you are the more you let people get into their own heads. I don't know if that's some kind of a rule that we've been taught, or just what it is, but I find that true with me. Like, I've always felt that real psychedelic music, for instance, could be found in the first Dylan albums

— PAUL: The more you channel your actions in one direction, the more force there is behind what you're doing. DAVID: Right. PAUL: I just want to watch out for people drawing the conclusion that the new Dylan album means you shouldn't have been playing all those instruments after all, which is just nonsense. If they listen to the Byrds album then they'll understand that, but . . . and that's what a lot of people think "simplicity" means. It's like vindication for all the guys with their guitars.

DAVID: I still think simplicity is the highest form of art. Simplicity is unique for each person who's involved in it; I mean there's no hard line as to what is simple; and what is simple to Brian is not necessarily simple for Dylan, and what is simple for him is not necessarily simple for the Stones, or the Doors . . . very funny, the other day Morrison made a comment that really made me feel good: his favorite musician is Brian Wilson. PAUL: Jim? DAVID: Mm-hm. PAUL: That's amazing. DAVID: And one of his favorite albums is *Wild Honey*. I mean he really got into it . . . And what was even more mind-blowing about that particular situation was that Jim immediately hipped, or I guess had always been hip to the fact of Brian's involvement with humor. We happened to get into a conversation about humor, and the importance of humor, and immediately Jim mentioned Brian. And *Wild Honey*. And I think he, I believe if I remember correctly he was talking about *Wild Honey* and Brian in terms of direct, forceful statements.

PAUL: Well, the Doors have done essentially only one thing in their whole career; the Doors have done what other people are figuring out how to do, in other words make single statements, unify everything, and make it all come out of that one piece of art. And the Doors' problem therefore has been that people waited for something else to happen, and didn't get it, and weren't always satisfied with more of the same great stuff. So it's going to be very interesting that they're now thinking about other things.

DAVID: It's very strange; and it seems that only in music we find this, this need to keep changing. I directly relate it to painting—we're in a situation right now where everybody has to be a Picasso, everyone has to get into new things with every painting. And uh . . . Rembrandt certainly had his one style, Modigliani had his one style, most of the recognized great painters pretty much stuck within the one style that they found to be their own. PAUL: There's a perfectly good reason: it's the newspaper aspect of rock. It just comes out, you know; a new album comes out three months, five months, after the last one, and you're conscious of it as a part of right now. Maybe you won't be ten years from now, but right now you're conscious that this is The New Album, and you're thinking that way. DAVID: Yeah, that makes a lot of sense to me. If the recording artist were in the same position as the painter, let's say, and recorded continually as the painter paints continually, I think that he would very quickly come to his particular thing and stay with it, whereas, you're right, recording an album right now is really an event. It's an event for the record label, it's an event for the artist, it's an event for the people who are waiting for the album. PAUL: Everybody goes through their little birth sequence. DAVID: Everyone thinks that this next one has to be something more than the last one. And I think we've really gone through it. It's just ridiculous, this fantastic searching that everyone goes through trying to come up with something new, as if that were important. PAUL: People are just beginning to settle down now.

Like I know what's happened to me: I've finished this book, or I will have when we finish this conversation, and I no longer . . . somehow, although I was never conscious that I felt it before, I now know that I don't feel any more responsibility—which I did—in terms of writing about rock and roll. I don't know to whom . . . But from now on I can sit down and anything I write about rock and roll is just for fun, for me; 'cause I've got other things to do, I've proven myself in this area. Whereas before . . . an example of this is I'm only now getting to the point where I don't feel I have to listen to everything that comes out that's good. I never listened to everything that came out, I never got into that hangup. But now I'll even know that a record is good, and I will get around to it; but if I feel like listening to nothing but old Who singles for the next two weeks, that's what I'll do. I don't worry about having people looking at me funny 'cause I don't know where it's at, or whatever.

Okay, so for a rock group, now, consider how difficult it has been to be in a field where you have to be a part of what's happening, and every month they change the rules. I think we might just now be getting to the point where a group can feel they don't have to do this or have to do that. Up to now, there were always responsibilities; and I think they were always vague and felt by the person rather than imposed from outside.

DAVID: And it's very strange, because Elvis has been there for eleven years, showing everyone that they didn't have to do anything that . . . he's been doing his one thing for eleven years! And they've been buying it. And every rock group has said "Yeah. Elvis. Elvis." You can't talk to any person in the music scene who doesn't hold Elvis at a certain level. And he's never changed. He's always been Elvis. And uh . . . And I think Brian is always gonna be Brian! I think Brian is really on the road now; that's why I'm anxious for his next album, 'cause I think the next album is gonna be the solidification of what he's been doing. *Pet Sounds* was *Pet Sounds;* and I think *Smile,* looking back now that I've gotten into *Wild Honey,* I think *Smile* would've been an extension of *Pet Sounds,* that Brian probably figured was not necessary.

PAUL: Ahh. I don't think you can use the word "necessary" in relation—that's another thing I mean about responsibility, the point at which we really start breathing a little easier, is the point at which we don't— DAVID: We don't put all the people on our shoulders. PAUL: All of a sudden we don't have to think that anything's necessary in terms of the art. DAVID: That's easy to trace with Brian. Until *Pet Sounds,* and everyone started paying attention to Brian, he was making music. He was making music that he felt he had to make, and all of a sudden he was surrounded by all these people who kept saying, "You're a leader, you've really got the responsibility, look what you're doing," and I think he got into that for a while. PAUL: And he did it to himself, too; he started thinking of *Pet Sounds* as a breakthrough, the work of a new person . . . DAVID: Well, he allowed himself to fall prey to what was going on, it was Othello and Iago, in a sense, and then all of a sudden I think he realized that that's not where he's at. Where he's at is to make the music that he wants to make, whatever it may be, whether it's "Help Me Rhonda" or "In My Room" or "God Only Knows" or whatever. "Darlin'." *Wild Honey.* When I listen to *Wild Honey* I really remember Brian sitting at that piano by himself just screaming his soul out. And he doesn't have to do any more than that. For anyone who likes Brian that's where it's at. *Wild Honey should* be celebrated. You were right.

PAUL: People have to relax. There are too many albums out right now to listen to, there's too much good music to appreciate, there are too many other things to do to be able to get your life in balance at all, in that way. I don't care if people read their issues of *Crawdaddy!* when they come out or six months later. I don't care how recently an album was released. This is not a letting go, it's a sitting back. DAVID: Sitting back and relaxing. PAUL: And as it starts influencing the business itself, it should really make a lot of musicians feel better.

DAVID: I think it's going to be very good for the business. Just in the few people that I associate with, they're more solid now into the area of recording albums that are musical, as opposed to the next major production album. There's a whole bunch of excitement going on, because everyone is really relaxing. I mean all the artists are now saying, "Thank god, we can get back to our music, we don't have to search and struggle and anticipate a $50,000, five-month-in-the-making record." And it's gonna be beautiful.

PAUL: What did you learn from Mike Love? DAVID: I didn't learn anything from Mike Love, I just learned something about Mike Love. I was at the last Love—this is a very funny thing, the way everything happened; we were cutting two more sides for what we thought at that time would be the next Love single. I was having my head blown sitting there, watching Love really getting it together, sounding better than they've ever sounded and being happier than I've ever seen them in a recording studio. And right in the middle of this, Mike Love and Al Jardine walked in, and I hadn't seen them in an awful long time.

I left the studio for a moment to talk to Mike and Al, and I noticed the fantastic physical difference in Mike, a real peace thing happening to him. He was very exuberant about his experiences with the Maharishi and transcendental meditation—which is something that I am not into nor do I really understand, except for the fact that I have talked to a lot of people lately who have been exposed to both the Maharishi and his philosophy and who have really changed, are really peaceful with themselves. And Mike was just bubbling over about the Beach Boys' involvement with the Maharishi and their plans to leave for India and also their plans for the tour that I believe they have now set up with the Maharishi.

But the incredible thing was the change in Mike. He was so calm, so quiet, so gentle and happy around the eyes and very genuine. The first thing that came to my mind while he was talking, as I was standing there listening to him, was the last time we were together doing the interview and I was talking about the negative things that used to go down between Brian and Mike. And I was wondering if that still existed or if they had found their niche together, 'cause Brian has been into the Maharishi for so long. I have no way at this point of knowing what that means . . . unless I can see them together. I'm waiting for Mike to come back 'cause he said we would get together when he came back and talk about some things. PAUL: It would seem that the Beach Boys are getting back together. DAVID: It sure seems that way, doesn't it? PAUL: Because I'm sure that the Beach Boys, the other Beach Boys are very happy with this album too. DAVID: I would think so. PAUL: It's the solution to a lot of problems.

I love the way we can see all sorts of answers now, and we couldn't see any, to the *Wild Honey* question, at the beginning, I mean when we were really looking. This has to do, I think, with what a breakthrough is. A breakthrough is really a move from two dimensions into three dimensions. DAVID: Well the last time we talked, when we heard *Wild Honey*, that was still very new to me . . . I guess I couldn't see the trees for the forest. I was expecting so much and it was all there but I didn't recognize it. And it took a couple of things to all of a sudden remember, and your phone conversation, and *John Wesley Harding* and watching this whole transitional thing happening and the going back and whatever it is that's going on. And all of a sudden realizing—

PAUL: This interview, to me—well, it's first of all of course a study of Brian Wilson, an attempt at evoking him for a lot of people, a look into who he is. And in the context of my book, the only deep look into who the artist is in relation to the music, an attempt to capture that. And it's full of dead ends; I mean I like it partly for that reason. DAVID: Yeah, there are a lot of dead ends. PAUL: Like we spent basically the first two installments as it appears in the magazine talking about how *Smile* got lost and what was gonna happen and in fact the end of the second installment is a cliff-hanger, you know about is Brian going to do it or not? Even though the answer was right in front of us. And what I would hope is that through this, that this interview would become for people like a story about not just who the artist is a little but who the listener is. DAVID: That would be beautiful, if the listener can be made aware of himself through anything that's happening here . . . it would be like the frosting on the cake.

PAUL: We're all listeners, which we forget, just like our economic system falls apart because we forget that we're all consumers. Everybody. It was supposed to work on that principle.

The same thing here, the artist is himself a listener—oh, we talked about Brian not listening to other people's records much and that sort of thing, but—let's not just say listener but . . . we don't have a word for it, a listener and a watcher, person-who-experiences . . . there's an intake, for instance we talked about Brian's— DAVID: A massive intake, I hope in the interview that that comes across, because as incredibly strong as he is in terms of output, he's equally strong in input. Just massive consumption, of the world and everything. When I said that Brian doesn't listen much, that was really erroneous on my part. He listens, he listens with simplicity, I mean he gets it immediately and he gets the whole thing right away, he gets it on mass consumption and just boom! he soaks it all in and it's digested and he listens the way I think we would like people to listen, everyone to listen. He doesn't listen with the critical thing up front, he just listens to whatever it is, just the way he sees things for whatever they are and then they form their, uh, whatever it is that forms is automatically formed.

PAUL: A number of years ago, at a time when I was still thinking of wanting to be a writer and all, I flashed on a concept of myself as wanting to do three things—experiencing, you know, taking in whatever was out there, understanding it, that's the second part, and then communicating it to people. And I recently came back to that, to that concept. You could talk about intake, digestion, and production.

DAVID: That really is so simple.

But how few people really get all those three things going equally. Most people try to concentrate on the middle thing, they try to understand everything without experiencing it, and then too few of them have the capacity or the knowledge of how to get it out, how to communicate it. PAUL: You know, I think the middle thing is the natural one, digestion is the natural one, so you can't figure out how to do it; that's why we're against interpretation or whatever. It's really simply because we know that if you've got things coming in the way you want them, good things are happening to you, you're getting involved in what you want to be involved in, and if you know what you want to produce, whether it's a kind of writing or music or whatever, then the link, digestion, you pretty much—it's what's called doing things by ear or sailing by the seat of your pants. You get very skilled at having things come in and then without really thinking about it moving them through your head, through your life, your artistic person towards the point where they come together and emerge as something whole. DAVID: A lot of people fake it. PAUL: Yeah, they take it in, and they let it sit there for a while, and then they toss it out. DAVID: Right, they don't try to understand it at all, and they don't even really take it all in, but they *try* to get it all out, they try to foist it upon everyone else.

PAUL: Well, you know what's a good essay on this subject? The liner notes of *John Wesley Harding*. DAVID: Oh, the liner notes of *John Wesley Harding*! I played the album so many times before I even got into the liner notes at all, I didn't even read them, and then one night I was walking into the kitchen and the album cover was sitting on the table and I grabbed it and just casually started reading it. And then I had to just sit down, and I got into that thing, and I was on the floor laughing. Such a beautiful thing to happen all of a sudden one dumb lonely night, to have that thing happen in my brain.

PAUL: Listening is another digestion operation, the concept of relaxing is a move towards understanding how to digest. Remember the Byrds' song "5D"? Where he talks about, "Just relax and feel it around you." DAVID: You can't really get it without relaxing. The work comes later; I think the work comes in between the knowledge and the output. You have to train yourself to observe, or train yourself to experience totally, to hear, it is definitely a training process. But after you as an individual get to that point, then you have to relax. Let it happen to you. PAUL: Let yourself function, because you've become some sort of a functioning thing, and you can just let it work.

Well, this is the—the relaxed part of the interview. DAVID: We've really digressed from Brian, haven't we? But he allows you to do that. (Laughter.) Brian allows you to go on your own trip. I would like to comment, though, before this is all over, about the picture you used in the first installment. I don't know how, who, what, or any of those situations on that picture, but that has to be the best picture I've ever seen of Brian. Ever. That's . . . so *perfect* for what was happening in that interview—that picture tied in with the very last thing we were talking about, which was, if you remember, the physical thing. Brian would always get that look on his face, or he'd always yawn—when it was time to stop talking about something, and he would want you to know that, he would yawn. And you knew after a while that, okay, it's all over, now we go play or something—he may catch you right in the middle of a sentence too, he'll yawn, that's all. Maybe tomorrow we'll pick up, but for right now, no more talk, time to do something. And it just blew my mind to see that particular picture. 'Cause that's so perfect. PAUL: Well, the way things happen is always very complicated and strange, and not always relevant to the fact that they do happen . . . that was the only photo available . . .

See, given that we have a new attitude towards the records now, as a result of *Wild Honey* and *John Wesley Harding* and whatever, and that we've progressed or broken through to the artist appreciating what he's doing, and us appreciating what's he's doing, on a much less self-conscious, formal kind of basis, a much more immediate basis, ah, something that's going to happen, whether we try to do it or not, is that we're going to change around our idea of who the artist is. That's "us" as listeners. In other words, the way that Bob Dylan would have been written about and thought of as a superstar at one time has already changed a great deal. But I don't think it's gotten to the point yet where anybody really has an exact idea of who Bob Dylan is. Which they did when he was a superstar—I'm not saying they were right, they had an exact idea, that's all. And probably in a few more months we'll all be well set in our new fantasy of who Bob Dylan is. The fantasy is unavoidable—the point is, our concept of who the artist is is changing. And what I want to do is sort of round off our story of Brian by going right at it and saying, your saying who Brian Wilson now seems to be.

DAVID: Brian now seems to be the Brian Wilson that I first met in the early days of "Good Vibrations," before it was finished, and also the same Brian Wilson that I knew from two o'clock in the morning to seven o'clock in the morning when it was just Brian and I sitting in the living room talking. It was the Brian Wilson away from all the hooplah, before he started perhaps listening to what people were saying about him. A very simple person, um . . . again, "simple," we get to that word . . . a very direct person, a person who really knew who he was, both as a person and as an artist. A person who had the incredibly complex mechanisms pretty much under control. He would go into a studio without fear, because he had confidence, in himself and in his art. He had things pretty much—he had everything in perspective, he had eliminated everything that was unnecessary. Brian was really —people used to really think Brian was a simple person in the true sense of the word simple, because he just didn't need all of the fooforall that a lot of us get hung up in, that we don't get hung up in any more, some of us . . . He was the artist, Brian was an artist, he was an artist who knew his art, as he is right now. PAUL: And then he discovered the word "artist." DAVID: Right.

Whatever agony, and god knows there is a lot with him, whatever loneliness, whatever indecision that goes on, that is necessary in a person like Brian, all that was safely tucked away inside of him, that was his own world. He had learned somewhere along the line how to keep that inside of him, and how to eliminate all those things in his surroundings that would cause him to lose control. I think he's there right now. I think he went through a terrible period, for a while, and then into a period of isolation, and then the clear light came to him and I think he has now gone back to where he was just previous to *Pet Sounds*. PAUL: Gone ahead to where he was. DAVID: And he must be very happy right now. He must be as happy as Brian Wilson can be happy. He's probably exploring all the numerous realms of humor, which is again his big thing. I don't think he's hung up.

That's the whole thing. Brian, when I first met Brian he was the most un-hung-up person I'd ever met. And that's why people couldn't relate to him, because it was during the time when you really had to be hung up to get it on, and Brian just was not. I don't think he's hung up now. He must be in the studio exactly the way he was then: just get in there and get it on, get it done, and get it out, and go on to the next thing. And that's what *Wild Honey* is to me, at this point. And "Darlin' " is just the essence of the Brian that I knew; it's doing the thing, it's doing his thing, it's doing Brian Wilson's thing. Come hell or high water, no concern really for what they out there think. It's what Brian Wilson thinks. He has to be grooving with the guys, and they have to be grooving with him again. It's gotta be a unified situation.

I don't know. You know, I try to relate Brian to other figures or other people, to try to get a comparison thing or some kind of a mirror thing happening . . . for some reason I keep coming up with images like Rembrandt. I don't know who the hell Rembrandt was, except for what we read and what we can get, or what I can personally get from looking at his works, collective works. An artist who is totally sure of what he is doing, who believes in what he is doing, who is conscious of what's going on around him, probably more conscious than the great mass of other people, but unconcerned while being concerned—not letting it get in his way. Being able to listen to someone else's music and say, "Yeah; all right." You know, "That's groovy. That's groovy for them. But I'm not in a competition scene with them, I'm doing my thing." And he is indeed doing his thing. And he's going to capture, or recapture, a lot of people. He's going to get a whole entire new audience, he's going to be able to get the new generation that's coming in now to the music thing, he's going to get back a lot of us old-timers . . .

And he's not concerned, he can't be concerned with his influence in the music business. Any guy who could dress the way Brian dressed, you *know* is not hung up with appearance, is not hung up with what others are doing. He's into his thing, whatever makes him comfortable he'll do. Whatever he wants to do at the moment. He doesn't have to sit and ponder and worry and get hung up and inactive because he's so strung out. He knows what's gonna happen and he's doing it. And in his doing it will be accomplished. It's an emancipation, an artistic emancipation that not many people have. It comes from confidence and it also comes from a kind of naive thing that artists have, good artists have; they're really naive. "Hey, my stuff is good." Which is beautiful. Without that, forget it. It's egoless, in terms of being a nonconscious thing . . .

PAUL: Brian, I think, is out of time. DAVID: Brian has *always* been out of time. PAUL: And, uh, *Smile* took the shape of a concept which then had to be realized. And its failure to happen, well it was the slip, 'twixt the cup, you know, it was between the, what is it, the desire and the spasm falls the shadow or whatever Eliot goes on about . . . but it was be-

cause . . . at some later point in Brian's career, at some moment of even greater capability than he has now, *Smile* could
have come to him and it would have gone right down. Well I
guess "Surf's Up" came to him and it went right down, only
then he didn't perceive it as being right down.

And delayed it, thought about it . . . DAVID: You just said
something that really flashed me. It has to happen *immediately,* with Brian, the idea comes to the mind and he understands it instantly. Instinctively understands it. If Brian has
to wait on something, pass. If he can't (snap fingers) get
it done like that, if he can't act upon it immediately and see
it happening in front of his eyes, it's not gonna work. If he
has to wait until morning, it's not gonna happen. That's what
happened with *Smile.*

Peter Townshend of The Who.
Photo by Ken Greenberg.

7: HOW ROCK COMMUNICATES

February 1968

"A great many considerations and puzzles that one meets sooner or later in all the arts find their clearest expression, and therefore their most tangible form, in connection with music."

—Suzanne K. Langer, *Feeling and Form*

"I know you deceive me; now here's a surprise . . ."

—Peter Townshend, "I Can See for Miles"

"I have never consciously written a song through a personal experience or an inspiration. I never write about things that happen to me. A lot of writers will say they did a song because they were in a certain mood but that's never happened to me. I can write happy when I'm sad or sad when I'm happy. I just get an idea and work on it."

—Smokey Robinson, interviewed in *Hit Parader*

I got up this morning and listened to "Heroes & Villains." Awakening from deep sleep, unconsciousness spills hesitantly away, aspects of the real slowly mixing in with the rest of your mind. "My children were raised you know they suddenly rise; it started slow long ago head to toe healthy, wealthy and wise . . ."* Last week I was at Van Dyke Parks's home in the

* Lyrics to "Heroes & Villains" Copyright © 1967 by Sea of Tunes Publishing Co.

Hollywood Hills; the week before, chatting with Brian Wilson at the Kennedy International Airport. He hadn't heard Van's album yet. He'd been surprised to read about *Smiley Smile* in *Crawdaddy!* When *Smiley Smile* came out, I wondered why "Heroes & Villains" didn't sound as good in stereo. Now I was listening to the single for the second time this morning. I stepped into the shower.

I don't know how I get these things on paper. Thoughts in my mind form words on a page through my fingers; concepts come together and generate ideas, and what can I point to to say, "I intended that"? The reader himself has no certain idea what goes on as his eyes touch the paper. He receives. I have given. But how?

How do we get from one place to another? (Now I'm thinking out loud.) Space is conquered by movement. Freedom of movement is granted by lack of restraint. There are things I can move through—water, and air; there are things that detain me, like stone. I cannot walk through fire. How do we get from one place to another? We will ourselves to move through receptive media.

Then what are our vehicles for? They get us there safer, and faster, retarding our movement in time. We cover more space and less time. What is a vehicle for an image, a concept? Something that carries that concept, from here to there, in space and time. I hear music in New York that was recorded in Oklahoma; I hear it today and tomorrow; the musicians performed it last year. And the music itself is a vehicle, just like my words on the page. Pick up a concept, stick it in the music, send it on its way.

The medium. The medium. It's all pretty complicated. The medium carries the message, but that's not all there is to it. Some people relate to Bob Dylan's vision of the world. That doesn't have anything to do with the medium, that's something that's in his head. And now it's in your head. The music —the medium—delivered it intact.

But suppose you say you relate to the music itself. Now

you're digging the package, right? But it's the music that communicates—the feeling you get from the melody, from the beat, from the sound of the words and all that interacting with the words themselves, the specific concepts. So maybe the package, the medium, *is* the message, since we can't quite separate Bob Dylan's vision from Bob Dylan's music. But . . . no, the music and the message aren't the same thing either. They aren't separable, but they aren't the same thing. You can't pry the painting from the canvas and the oils, but that doesn't mean the materials *are* the painting. Just a minute, Mr. McLuhan.

Communication is transportation (uh, I'm just fooling around here; I wouldn't want to perpetrate *new* slogans). Time and space are things to pass through, art is the rearranging of the universe into patterns reflecting the artist's will. Message is a specific thing, a discernible thing. Will is not. Few artists deal with messages, few artists expect you to go at the physical body of their work with a scalpel and attempt to extract its essence. The artist's emotions and sense perceptions are transmitted by means of his work. He receives, and he sends so that you may receive. The medium is not important. The medium is inanimate, an object. What you receive—not a message, not a specific, but a sum of messages, an emotion, a vision, a perception—what you receive is a part of the artist. It's alive. It's reborn in you. Music. The notes are not important. Virtuosity means nothing. No one cares how well you rearrange the objects. You gotta have soul, baby, which just means it's gotta be *you* you're passing on, people receiving parts of people, living matter, animate stuff. The medium *and* the messages it contains are just so much nothing, trees falling in the forest with no one to hear, unless there is human life on both ends of the line, sending, receiving, transferring bits of human consciousness from one soul to another. Communication is the interaction between our personal worlds.

Stepping out of the shower, I put on the Byrds.

Dear Trina:

That song by the Who, "I Can See for Miles," has meant more and more to me lately. I hear it in my mind. The song explodes in bursts of energy, from my brain, through my body, down the street by which I'm walking and out into the world, pulling me with its strength towards infinity. Peter Townshend's guitar rings harder and faster, and I can feel for centuries.

I first heard the song in September, thinking: "Ah. Hard rock. But not so advanced for the Who . . ." It sounded like an exceptional performance of an unexceptional work, and I let it go at that. And then in October, all my jealousy and rage, the song rediscovered as a vent for my passion, earphones and violence "miles and miles and miles and miles and miles . . ."

November, Los Angeles, the Who on all the radios, especially one blasting moment of Proustian significance in the backseat of Rothchild's rented car, suddenly *the* record of the year, all meaning, all truth to my cross-country crossed-wires mind. You may take one giant step. Rock and roll has entered the realm of forever . . .

You know what I mean, that special feeling after the last words of a book, that goes on and on extending that book and yourself across forever into now, the sudden unexpected sense of the real, the flash of power and together, in your mind. Perhaps something slips in Einstein's continuum, and for one quite certain moment you taste another level—we all know the desperate need to sustain that. And Townshend's achievement is somewhere along these lines.

But this is emotion, and you have asked me to explain. The last day in LA, you wondering, "What does the music mean to you? What is it that you hear in it, how do you react?" I want to tell you, you have a need to know; but I wonder how far that question reaches, if even one book is enough to begin to answer it . . .

Recently some girl told me, while I rapped about the future of the universe, that she hadn't been able to think so far lately, it had been like a wall before her mind, and although now she got a little distance . . .

You remember how on Jane Street I couldn't write at all, only for deadline and even then I preferred my office; and moving up here has meant tens of thousands of words, something every day? It's because I can see the river, because looking out the window I have a feeling of open space, cars and lights below me, buildings, boats, New Jersey stretched beyond. My mind is open, free. I have a horizon. I can see for miles . . .

And the power of the song is all in musical perspective: if you sketch the railroad tracks you see them going on forever, there in your little ten by twelve frame, and Townshend not only makes you hear forever, there in his four-minute song, but pulls you into it, puts you out there with the immediacy, and involvement that is rock. Kineticism was always limited, it couldn't really go on beyond the orgasm; but Pete discovered that as in sex the perfect union knows no timing, so in music you could direct that feeling, paint the railroad tracks just so . . .

And then last week I called it the song of the revolution; I didn't know why. Often a comment will come for no reason, just a feeling, a flash of future thought before it happens, the time machine in operation, a chunk of next week now.

But revolution to me is ecological, the big world move towards human sense; and I was carrying on about my vision of what could be when this girl made her comment on her thinking, and, indirectly, on mine. Distance . . . thinking as a spatial function . . . looking out across the river and opening my mind . . . It all came together, I don't know why I didn't connect these things before, the ability to think about the future and the freedom to see for miles and miles and miles and miles and miles . . . oh yeah . . .

And Townshend's song, which seemed about unfaithfulness back when that was foremost in my mind, could now become for me a statement to my world: "I know you deceive me, now here's a surprise—I know that you do 'cause there's magic in my eyes—a joke on you, you're gonna choke on it too, you're gonna lose that smile because all the while I can see for miles and miles"* . . . the ecological revolution, Frank Herbert's *Dune*, the need for incredible visionary perception that we may see all the contexts, put the world in perspective and work to straighten it out . . . Oh yes, it's my trip and not necessarily Townshend's (or Dylan's? "Let us not speak falsely now . . ."), but maybe this tells you something about what I hear in the music, how it affects me, the level it communicates on . . .

Anyway, I've been listening to "River Deep Mountain High" and feeling it everywhere and thinking about you. See you soon.

Love,
Paul

The Byrds go right at it. They are about as nice as you could be and still seem absolutely real, and few of us could think of groups we'd rather listen to. It's always what's there on the record that's stunning; not the quality or the cleverness of what's there, not the music or the intent of what's there, but the stuff itself—you hear it and you react, you feel good, you understand, you are entirely and personally involved. First you think: "Wow. I really love the Byrds," and then you maybe stop to think about why you love them or what it is that you think is so good. Maybe you never even know, but the important thing is, they always get to you.

Anyway, they always get to me. And I have a lot of friends who for maybe a month after any given Byrds album comes out walk around muttering "wow" and saying that when they really think about it, the Byrds are their very favorite rock group. And then they forget for a while, until another Byrds record appears; and of course it's not thinking about the

Byrds that impresses them but hearing the Byrds. And isn't this how it should be?

The Byrds more than anybody today have mastered communication. Part of it is that they're not afraid. Not on any of the important levels. They try, but they're not very conscious of what they're "supposed to be" doing, and this is a saving grace. Such an ominous toy as the Moog becomes in their hands just a thing to make sound with at the beginning of "Natural Harmony." They aren't intimidated. They're in control, the music is completely theirs, there is no distance between man and machine because machine is appreciated as simply tool, extension of man, something to do things with. The same is true of the horns, strings, everything on *The Notorious Byrd Brothers*. The listener is absolutely not aware of strings on "Going Back," not because he can't hear them—they're right there—but because he's hearing the song. In the best art you cannot see the artist's handiwork. You can only feel his presence, in what you're perceiving, you're overwhelmed by that and not concerned with examining it. You relate. Sex can be much closer, more direct, than we think the word "close" means. So can looking at Picasso. So can listening to the Byrds.

Now that we are ready, now that they are ready, the Byrds do not ignore specifics. It is just the right time to sing about amphetamine, in the context of Memphis brass and waves of nonfeeling; it is just the right time to follow that with further reflections on an overthought theme, going back, younger than yesterday, my back pages, underthought this time: a little bit of courage is all we lack, I'm going back. That means less and feels more. Vietnam is on this album. Vietnam is everywhere these days. Last year it would not have been proper; last year Vietnam and rock were not so close for us, we couldn't have made the bridge. This year some things are in all things, and the Byrds are us too, they feel that too, and what they feel is what's present on this album.

There is a natural progression, in my mind, from the Love album (*Forever Changes*) to the Dylan album (*John Wesley Harding*) to *The Notorious Byrd Brothers*. Self-awareness is the word I like to use, the artist aware of who he is and putting it right across, no distance, just presence. Horns, steel guitars, strings, rock stuff, harmonies, melodies, words ideas concepts phrasing are all part of it, all more and more natural and invisible as the person of the artist takes shape, takes form, becomes present in the living room or wherever you listen, wherever you hear. Talking to a friend on the telephone, you get only voice, some words in straight-line order, inflection of voice, and a lot of memory, a lot of consciousness of who this person is from all you knew before. Listening to the Byrds, you have heard all those other albums, you know what you know, and you also have words in multileveled order, inflections, melodies and rhythms, every sort of rich communication directly to/with you.

On a Byrds album how much distance is there between what the artist (several people, but singular on records) is trying to do and what he does? None at all, or not perceptible, or maybe we don't care what he was *trying* to do. He must have been trying to do this, he *did* this and it's incredible. No distance. Does this mean the medium's the message? No. Both those things are impersonal. This is all personal. The Byrds is the Byrds. The music and the group are the same concept, the same thing in our minds, the same thing on the record; the people are not the same as the music, but then the people in the Byrds are not the same as the Byrds, which is part of why they come and go so much. The Byrds is a true gestalt, successful insofar as six great albums and fifty-nine songs have been produced by that gestalt, successful insofar as that gestalt is known as a person to more people than most individuals are.

There is no distinction in time between Byrds albums; more than any other group they are as good on their first album, as appropriate now on their first album as they are now on this album, and I suspect this album would have sounded perfectly fine back then, three years ago. The Byrds are now, the Byrds have always been now. They don't just say those things, they feel them, they get in and around and through all those things they say and no one but the Byrds has more right to say, "Just like the day of birth our first awakening to this earth" and "That which is not real does not exist." "Dance to the day when fear is gone." The Byrds have abolished time, for themselves, and for us all if we listen enough.

I'm really enthusiastic about this stuff. You could do me no greater favor than to read *Dune* and listen to the Byrds, be and grow well and perhaps communicate yourself when you are ready for it. Perhaps you're communicating now, and you'd forgotten. Remember the Byrds. They go right at it.

I'd like to review a book. You can get it in paperback. It's called *The Musical Experience,* the author's name is Roger Sessions, and you get it from Atheneum Books or the Princeton University Press. Roger Sessions is a composer, and a professor of music at Princeton; he must also be a very fine man, because his book is not only brilliant but completely reasonable, and there are very few reasonable men writing on music or anything else these days. (The book was written in 1950; but there was quite a lot of confusion in the air even then.)

What Mr. Sessions does, in these lectures prepared for his students, is to concern himself with what music really is to people; and he divides people, for the purposes of a discussion of music, into composers, performers, and listeners. "In the beginning, no doubt, the three were one. Later . . . the composer existed precisely because he had introduced into the raw material of sound and rhythm patterns that became recognizable and therefore capable of repetition. . . . The first performer was, in the strictest sense, the first musician who played or sang something that had been played or sung before. . . . Listening to music is the product of a very late stage in musical sophistication. . . . For the listener, music is no longer an incident or an adjunct but an independent and self-sufficient medium of expression."

The extent to which almost everything Sessions says about music in the abstract is applicable to rock music in particular is a healthy indication of the growth of rock into a modern art form, a lasting means of expression. And I would think that anyone who has read this far in *Outlaw Blues* would find *The Musical Experience* a fascinating and valuable work. Let me stop reviewing this book at this point, then, and instead report for you on that aspect of Mr. Sessions's approach, which is most incredible and illuminating in terms of what I have been trying to talk about. Let me give you Roger Sessions on time:

I am deliberately restricting the discussion here to primitive, direct, and simple responses to music. Even at this level, may we not say that the basic ingredient of music is not so much sound as movement, conceived in the terms I have indicated? I would even go a step farther, and say that music is significant for us as human beings principally because it embodies movement of a specifically human type that goes to the roots of our being and takes shape in the inner gestures which embody our deepest and most intimate responses. This is of itself not yet art; it is not yet even language. But it is the material of which musical art is made, and to which musical art gives significance.

If we appreciate these facts, we can understand the more readily why music is the art of sound. For of all the five senses, the sense of hearing is the only one inexorably associated with our sense of time. The gestures which music embodies are, after all, invisible gestures; one may almost define them as consisting of movement in the abstract, movement which exists in time but not in space. . . .

and, later in the book,

It is interesting to consider how many of our technical terms apply originally to things seen rather than things heard, or to space rather than time. The word "form" or "architecture," for example, led to the once famous comparison of the sonata form with an arch. . . . The real flaw in such a comparison is in the fact that what we call "form" in the realm of time has nothing whatever to do with, and is in no real way comparable to, "form" as we know it in the realm of space. The one is fluid, and its essence is fluidity; the other is static, and its primary requirement is stability.

Wow. Fluidity is of course available to the painter, to the visual artist dealing in any way with textures, but only the mobile arts can work from reference points in time. And only the visual arts can employ reference points in space. So the use of fluidity, movement, contrasts, repetition is very much an aspect of the medium in which the artist is working. Contrast, for example, is a fairly sophisticated technique in music, since it requires that the listener be involved enough to retain in his mind the events of one moment while listening to the events of the next. Hence the use of the first verse, second verse, break pattern in many rock songs—you have to get the listener used to something before you can effectively surprise him. Repetition, on the other hand, is as immediate in music as contrast is in painting—the orderly procession of a song in time really makes the word "cumulative" significant. Two great examples: Johnny Cash's "I Walk the Line," in which the absolutely unchanging guitar pattern, repeated throughout the song, creates affirmation; and the Rolling Stones' "Last Time," in which repetition of an unchanging guitar phrase is again used, but this time to create an atmosphere of doubt, uncertainty on a cosmic level. The key to the effectiveness of the guitar in each of these songs is its relationship to what's occurring in the vocal: in "I Walk the Line" the vocal is calm and constant, and the guitar backs it up; in "Last Time" Jagger shouts and pleads and cajoles and threatens, and the unresponsiveness of the guitar just becomes more and more ominous.

Film, ballet, drama are arts that employ both space and

time; and there has been constant conflict in these arts (as in all others) between the artist's desire for freedom and his need for security. The greatest art has often been created by men who were severely and specifically limited in what they could do, but who did not feel that this in any way restricted or limited their ability to express themselves. Music has always had its advantages in this respect, as it is an art form absolutely incapable of spatial expression (save to the extent that it can be louder or softer within a given area) and therefore rather seriously restricted from the outset. The further limit imposed by Top 40 radio (the birthplace and childhood home of rock music), that a song not exceed three or four minutes in length, has allowed artists who might otherwise be far too ambitious with far too little experience to really express themselves within a limited (from an objective point of view) form that is really (to the fledgling artist) as unlimited as any form of papyrus would be to the man who'd been trying to express himself by drawing in the air.

At this stage in its history, rock is bursting forth from restrictions placed on it in childhood, and I suppose we can say it is having a brilliant, though difficult, adolescence. It is discovering, in new ways every day, just what is really going on out here; and every new discovery is heralded as the final, unassailable truth. And perhaps (I hear it in the most recent music of the Kinks, the Who, the Byrds, the Beach Boys, Dylan) rock is just now beginning to discover that there are no unassailable truths, there is only greater and greater awareness of the universe. And of oneself.

In which case, Roger Sessions's is a good book to read. We have reached the stage where we know we're making music.

Let's take another approach to this thing. My friend Bhob Stewart suggests that after *Bringing It All Back Home* Dylan stopped calling his songs "Bob Dylan's 115th Dream" because he'd realized that *all* the songs were dreams, chains of seemingly related and unrelated sense perception, stories told through the mind's attempt to connect all the worlds it perceives. "My songs are only dreams," says Donovan, "visiting my mind." Dylan, who isn't so explicit, would probably not say "only." But he tells us his feelings on interpretation: "At dawn my lover comes to me and tells me of her dreams, with no attempts to shovel the glimpse into the ditch of what each one means ["How far would you like to go in?" asked Frank] . . . at times I think there are no words but these to tell what's true; and there are no truths outside the gates of Eden."*

Dreams and insight are equally involved in waking. "Sunshine came softly through my window today . . ." Donovan, sitting on his bed, can find the world a very certain place. He's bright-eyed enough to make visiting his mind a highly smileable experience. Dylan, though he's gentle—"these visions of Johanna have kept me up past the dawn"—can be a frightening cuss to wake up to. Frightening because of what he says ("The foes will rise with the sleep still in their eyes and they'll jerk from their beds and think they're dreaming") —what he sees ("They're selling postcards of the hanging") —and what he does: "I put my fingers against the glass and bowed my head and cried."

Jim Morrison, in concert before singing "Light My Fire," turns to the audience and screams "WAKE UP!" Which is funny, because I doubt that anyone thinks it a direct command (save Jim)—nothing about the Doors sticks out enough to require special attention, and "Wake up!" is just perceived as another part of what's there, whether the person is there or not. The Doors make so many demands on their listeners that everyone either dislikes them without knowing why or else assumes that anyone as great as the Doors doesn't merely expect you to follow their directions. The Doors are so thoroughly successful that "Wake up!" is always just part of the show.

Meanwhile, on what level of consciousness do we find

* Copyright © 1965 by M. Witmark & Sons.

Jody Reynolds? "Endless Sleep" (Demon Records FF-1507) was a hit in the fifties which Jody wrote himself (with Dolores Nance), all about Jody's melodramatic baby, who walked into the sea after a lover's quarrel. There's a lot going on here. "The night was black, rain falling down; looked for my baby, she's nowhere around. Traced her footsteps down to the shore—'fraid she's gone for ever more." The beat is as unemotional as Jody's voice. "I looked at the sea and it seemed to say, 'I took your baby from you away.' I heard a voice crying from the deep, 'Come join me baby in my endless sleep.' "*

The Doors' "Moonlight Drive" comes to mind. But more than that, notice how the chorus ends in the title of the song. This is the creation of drama from the totally expected. Death—an everyday, once-in-a-lifetime companion—is pretty exciting to your 1950's teen-age rock fan; and words that imply that somebody actually *died* are a source of great tension and vicarious pleasure in a pop-rock context. So here we have this song with its verse-chorus, verse-chorus, verse-chorus construction, and inevitably, like taxes, at the end of each chorus we're gonna get the death sentence, Jody is going to say "endless sleep." And he does. At the end of the third verse he even refers to "*that* endless sleep," which goes to show that the concept is an old friend by now. Historical tragedies work the same way—you *know* what's going to happen at the end (of the play, of the chorus), but each time you get really tense believing that somehow the impossible will occur, the inevitable will be avoided, whoever it is will be saved.

Redemption is a familiar theme in early rock (unlike historical tragedies), so you can bet that Jody saved his girl. There's still a tense moment when he's found her and holds her to him, and you don't know until the chorus if this is necrophilia. But the last line is "I saved my baby from that

* Copyright © 1957 by Johnstone-Montei, Inc.-Elizabeth Music.

endless sleep"; and notice how, redemption or no redemption, the chorus ends in the same fatal phrase. In fact, in some sort of wry emotionless comment on the whole thing, Jody ends the song by saying "endless sleep" about six times; and the last thought you have before going down is that, repeated, "endless sleep" becomes "endlessly." The rest is silence. And Bob Dylan says (*11 Outlined Epitaphs*), "Anything that ain't got no end's just gotta be poetry one way or another."

But do you suppose there could be a more than coincidental relationship between waking, sleeping, dreaming, and the creative process? The Everly Brothers once posed the immortal question: what happens if you really did fall asleep at the movies, and nobody will believe you? How do you prove you weren't fucking? In a society that speaks only in euphemisms ("sleep together," as the Beach Boys almost dare to say in "Wouldn't It Be Nice") and communicates only in excuses, what do you do with the truth? Wake up, little Suzie, wake up. It's a funny but desperate song.

And then there's the Four Tops' masterpiece, "Shake Me, Wake Me," a song almost too real and terrifying to be listened to. "All through this long and sleepless night I hear my neighbors talking (she don't love him). They say that out of my life and to another's arms you'll soon be walking. . . . Somebody shake me! Wake me! when it's over (when it's over); somebody tell me that I'm dreaming and wake me when it's over (when it's over). . . . They say our love ain't what it used to be, and everyone knows but me; I've closed my ears my forty-two years but the words are loud and clear. And through these walls so thin I hear my neighbors when they say that she don't love him. . . ." and "If I've ever ever dreamed before, somebody tell me I'm dreaming now. . . ."* It is said that the most frightening thing about LSD is that for some people the "trip" recurs long after

* Copyright © 1966 by Jobete Music.

you're off the drug. That hasn't happened to me; but certainly the most frightening thing about "reality" is that sometimes you can't get rid of it.

And maybe you never never did dream before, maybe your mind can pull greater tricks on you than you think, maybe time and memory and waking and sleeping are so very mixed up, and the mind so very inaccessible, that certain silly rock songs are the closest we can come to knowing reality.

"Shake Me, Wake Me" nicely ties together the subject matter of dreams and waking with the theme of illusion versus reality. The singer wants someone to wake him later, but he's awake; he has closed his ears but he (now) hears everything that's said around him. Reality is on and can't be turned off. Tommy James and the Shondells pull the reverse trick on their listeners in a song called "Mirage"; the mere fact of Tommy exclaiming, over your transistor radio or whatever, "just a mirage," is enough to make the radio, the song, and perhaps a good part of the afternoon vanish off the face of the Earth. Just how real is a song on the radio to any given listener? If the song's singer disclaims its reality, isn't that enough to tip the balance? . . . Being *able* to turn off reality is also a pretty frightening number.

Except, of course, when practiced by the Beatles. The universally loved, always palatable Beatles couldn't frighten their way out of a wet paper bag, and anyway they prefer to take the attitude that this is a groovy bag to be in: ". . . and after all, I'm only sleeping." No one threatens their reality, because they refuse to really care about what's real and what is not. "Turn off your mind, relax and float downstream." Or, alternatively, "Shake it up baby, twist and shout!" "Nowhere you can be that isn't where you want to be, it's easy" (if you take that attitude. Those of us who actually can remember being places we would rather never be again may wonder at the Beatles' absolutely indiscriminate absorption of the world. They consume more bulk than forty generations of rabbits, and manage to produce almost as much in return;

and these are extremely admirable, though unenviable, accomplishments). Doubts about reality, fear of the dark, are all very well for lesser rock groups; the Beatles are unshakable, which certainly contributes no end to their position as culture heroes, though it may someday detract from their standing as artists. There really isn't much distance between "Close your eyes and I'll kiss you" and "Living is easy with eyes closed"; and if there is any distance the Beatles will be glad to make it up for you. They really have homogenized their universe. "With my eyes wide open, I'm dreaming . . ."

"Before you slip into unconsciousness," begins Jim Morrison. "I gotta dream on," says Herman of the Hermits; and, "All I've got to do is dream; dream, dream, dream," says Don or Phil Everly. Morrison comes back with "Realms of the earth; realms of light; some are born to sweet delight; some are born to sweet delight; some are born to the endless night."* Oh yeah, almost forgot the birth theme. Frank Herbert writes a novel called *Do I Wake or Dream?* Berkley Books retitles it *Destination: Void.*

But does arbitrarily relating all these songs and things through their common subject matter really get us anywhere? Good question, but—how do we usually relate things? What does get us anywhere? This is *my* thought dream I'm spinning out for you; how does *your* chain of perception link together?

DYLAN: I am about to sketch You a picture of what goes on
    around here sometimes. tho I don't understand too well my-
    self what's really happening.

DONOVAN: What goes on? I really want to know.

DYLAN: I know no answers an no truth
    for absolutely no soul alive
    I will listen t no one
    who tells me morals
    there are no morals
    an I dream alot.

* Copyright © 1967 by Nipper Music.

A dream is a portrait, moving target for the mind. Waking is the shift from one level to another; here to there but not in space or time. This stuff is all important. And the hell of it is, rock really does communicate. It discusses this stuff in its own peculiar ways, and many an idea comes and goes without a conscious thought. Shifting, moving, existing, gone.

"Music is your special friend, dance on fire as it intends, music is your only friend ["When you hear music, after it's over, it's gone in the air and you can never capture it again." —Eric Dolphy] until the end, until the end, until The End." ("You know the day destroys the night . . .")*

And more. How rock communicates is a mystery to me. Some days I stand in the shower till evening, pushing at songs in my mind.

"I've been in this town so long, so long to the city . . ." (Van Dyke calls from the Coast; just wants me to know it's all right.) "I'm thick with the stuff" water running down the drain counterclockwise "to ride in the rough" Hudson Day River at an end "And sunny down snuff I'm all right

"By the heroes and villains . . ."

* Copyright © 1967 by Nipper Music.

Discography

CHAPTER 1
After Bathing at Baxter's, Jefferson Airplane, RCA VICTOR RECORDS
Their Satanic Majesties Request, The Rolling Stones, LONDON
    RECORDS
Beach Boys' Party, CAPITOL RECORDS

CHAPTER 2
Sunshine Superman, Donovan, EPIC RECORDS
Buffalo Springfield, ATCO RECORDS
The Byrds' Greatest Hits, COLUMBIA RECORDS

CHAPTER 3
Blonde on Blonde, Bob Dylan, COLUMBIA RECORDS
John Wesley Harding, Bob Dylan, COLUMBIA RECORDS

CHAPTER 5
The Doors, ELEKTRA RECORDS
"Blowing in the Wind," Bob Dylan, COLUMBIA RECORDS (available
    on *The Freewheelin' Bob Dylan,* COLUMBIA RECORDS, and
    Bob Dylan's Greatest Hits, COLUMBIA RECORDS)

CHAPTER 6
Pet Sounds, The Beach Boys, CAPITOL RECORDS
Smiley Smile, The Beach Boys, BROTHER RECORDS
Wild Honey, The Beach Boys, CAPITOL RECORDS

CHAPTER 7
"I Can See for Miles," The Who, DECCA RECORDS (available on
    The Who Sell Out, DECCA RECORDS)
The Notorious Byrd Brothers, The Byrds, COLUMBIA RECORDS
"Heroes and Villains," The Beach Boys, BROTHER RECORDS (avail-
    able on *Smiley Smile,* BROTHER RECORDS)
"Endless Sleep," Jody Reynolds, DEMON RECORDS
"Shake Me, Wake Me," The Four Tops, MOTOWN RECORDS (avail-
    able on *The Four Tops' Greatest Hits,* MOTOWN RECORDS)

Bibliography

Dune, Frank Herbert, ACE BOOKS
V., Thomas Pynchon, BANTAM BOOKS
The Crying of Lot 49, Thomas Pynchon, BANTAM BOOKS
More Than Human, Theodore Sturgeon, BALLANTINE BOOKS
The Musical Experience, Roger Sessions, ATHENEUM BOOKS

Recommended Reading

Avatar, 80 Wooster Street, New York, N.Y. 10012 ($5 for 12 issues)

Billboard, 2160 Patterson St., Cincinnati, Ohio 45214 ($20 for 52 issues)

Crawdaddy!, 383 Canal Street, New York, N.Y. 10013 ($5 for 12 issues)

Hit Parader, Charlton Publishing Corporation, Derby, Connecticut 06418 ($3.50 for 12 issues)

Rolling Stone, 746 Brannan Street, San Francisco, California 94103 ($6 for 26 issues)

Rock for Beginners

Sunshine Superman, Donovan, EPIC
Rubber Soul, Beatles, CAPITOL
Live in Europe, Otis Redding, VOLT
Electric Music for the Mind & Body, Country Joe & The Fish, VANGUARD
Procol Harum, DERAM
Greatest Hits Volume II, Smokey Robinson & The Miracles, TAMLA
Forever Changes, Love, ELEKTRA
Pet Sounds, The Beach Boys, CAPITOL
Mr. Tambourine Man, The Byrds, COLUMBIA

Song Cycle, Van Dyke Parks, WARNER BROTHERS
Between the Buttons, The Rolling Stones, LONDON
Something Else, The Kinks, REPRISE
Happy Jack, The Who, DECCA
Blonde on Blonde, Bob Dylan, COLUMBIA
Jefferson Airplane Takes Off, RCA VICTOR
Strange Days, The Doors, ELEKTRA
Four Tops Greatest Hits, MOTOWN
Earth Opera, ELEKTRA
Got Live If You Want It, The Rolling Stones, LONDON
Buffalo Springfield Again, ATCO

Background

The Buddy Holly Story, CORAL
Chuck Berry's Greatest Hits, CHESS
King of the Delta Blues, Robert Johnson, COLUMBIA
The Very Best of the Everly Brothers, WARNER BROTHERS
The Best of Muddy Waters, CHESS